AF231225

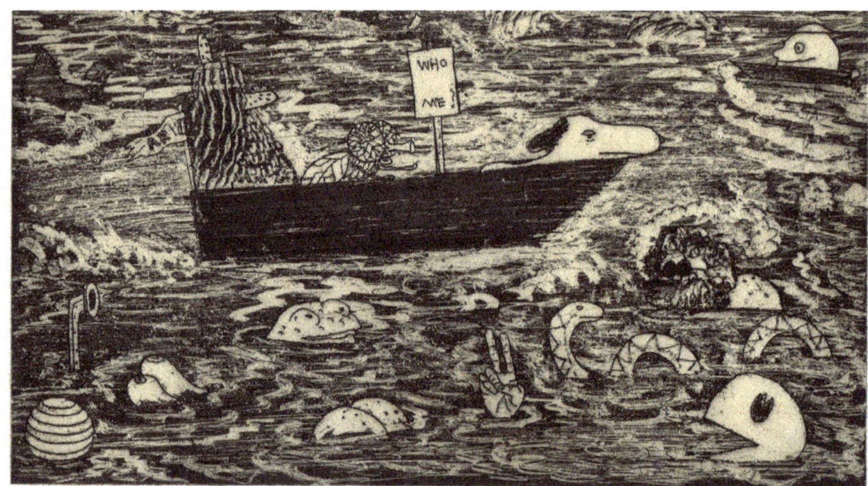

Michael Krueger
Who Me? River Styx
Intaglio,
Image size – 13" x 9"
paper size 18" x 14"
2015
ed. 7

photo courtesy of the artist

Chameleon Press
Kansas City, MO
http://chameleonartskc.org/
2nd Edition: 11 7 5 3 2 1
copyright © 2018 Hugh Merrill

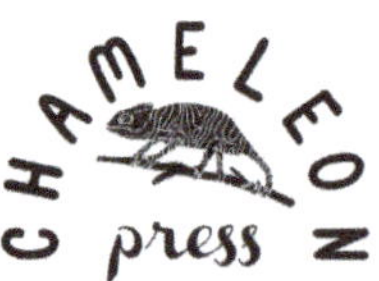

ISBN: 978-0-999-02222-1
Library of Congress Control Number: 2018932274

1st Edition:
Copyright © 2017 Chameleon Arts & Youth Development
First Edition 2017
ISBN: 978-0-692-56737-1

Proofreader: Susan Fiorello

All images in book courtesy of Chameleon photo archives unless otherwise noted.

PREACHING TO THE CHOIR

MERRILL
LEMON
POWERS

TABLE OF CONTENTS

ACKNOWLEDGEMENTS

My thoughts that make up these excursions into contemporary print-making were generated by discussions over beer or wine on many occasions. Visiting artist gigs, long discussions on the telephone prior to cell phones, participation in conference panels and exhibition invitations all played an important role. These writings were stimulated by the brilliance and insight of others so the substance contained here is only partly my own.

The history of contemporary printmaking is the story of artists and intellectuals on the outside of the mainstream and sometimes ignored, disrespected or misrepresented. Yet they simply keep making art, inventing new paths, expanding the traditions and engaging in foolishness as needed. A friend, Willie Birch, once asked me why I cared so much about printmaking and why I would spend (or waste) my time writing about it. For him, it was a discipline of techniques of no particular intellectual interest, for me it was a door that had opened allowing me a voice, a life, a means of individual expression, supported by a dynamic community. Yes, I am preaching to the choir and our congregation is small, but without it print would not be an international community of active creative brilliance.

I want to thank Ken Kerslake who took me in and taught me the importance of being in the community of print artists. As I write these names in the following list I know there are many good friends and members of the community left out but with each of you there is a story of gratitude and amazing respect: Eleanor Erskine, Beauvais Lyons, Steve Murakishi, Doug Baker, David Jones, Lynne Allen, Phyllis McGibbon, Ruth Weisberg, Frances Myers, Debra Wye, Ruth Fine, Mel Chin, Jim Leedy, Dennis McNett, John Hitchcock, Tom Huck, the Outlaw Printmakers and many others.

Many thanks to my book designer Shelby Lemon for her help on this project, it was much longer than I thought it would be.

Chameleon Arts wishes to thank the following organizations for their support: the Francis Families Foundation, the R.A. Long Foundation, the Lawrence A. and Joan S. Weiner Foundation, the ArtsKC Fund, the National Endowment for the Arts, the Missouri Arts Council and many individual donors.

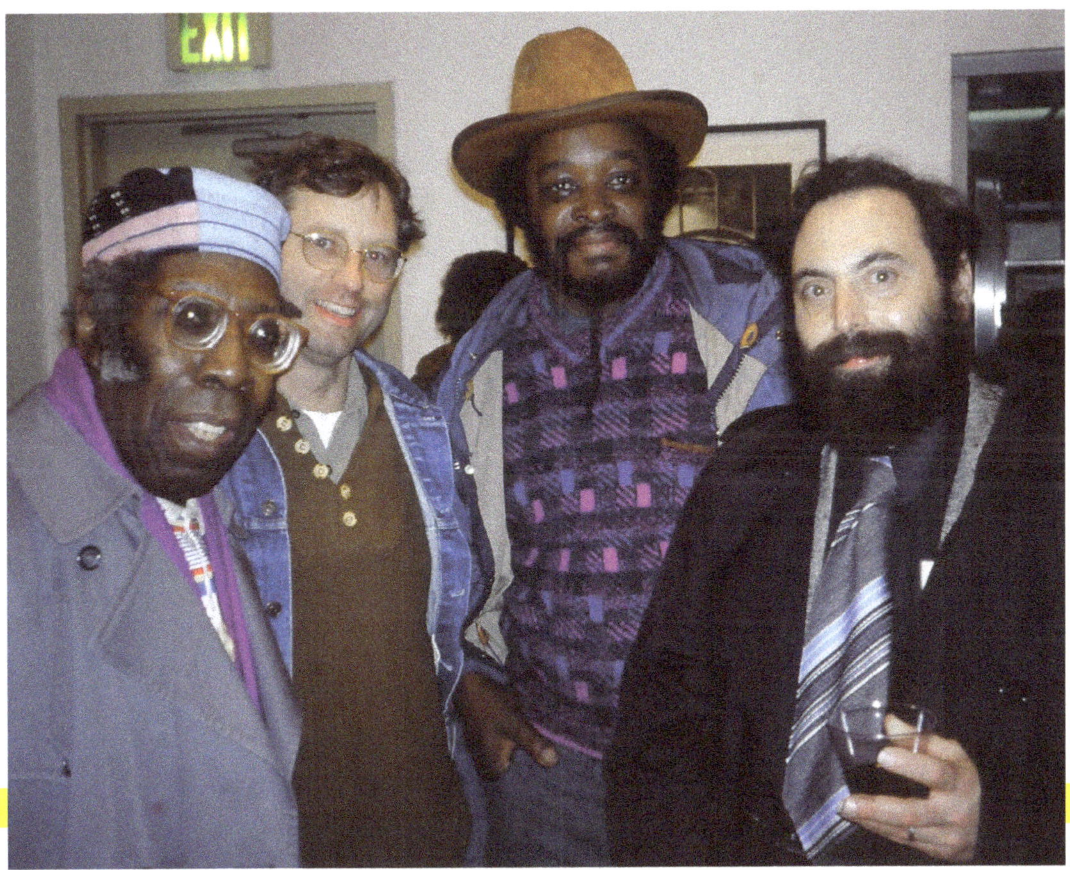

Robert Blackburn and Friends, 1993.

INTRODUCTION

 I saw Hugh Merrill, he was bouncing up and down in his seat and grinning from ear to ear about my presentation, which was on the role of community building in the Kansas City poetry scene peppered with some humor about my anarchist tendencies. He knew immediately what I would come to find out over the next two years: we would work together fantastically. We both share a deep joy of life and an immense energy to suck as much marrow as our skeletons can create.

Together, we've staged performance art events, held creative writing workshops, ran Chameleon Arts non-profit, issued grants to a number of stunning local activist artists, created Chameleon Press, walked our dogs and attended countless open mics where inevitably everyone is a bit thrown off and laughing about our shared chaotic approach to performance. We produced and published his first ever poetry book, *Nomadic? Rover by Days Singing These Gang Plank Songs of the Ambler* with 39 West Press. The book is fully illustrated in a way that causes the words to be interacting with the drawings continuously, which is perfect for Merrill's natural manic gregariousness.

My favorite collaboration was when Merrill and I developed "A Moment's Peace," an interactive poetic performance featuring the voices and talents of five women. The group began by creating an energy of dissonance in the air which rose to a crescendo of the pain of injustice and then established the slow process of dismantling the rage and shame into acceptance and action. The video projections changed from the Deep Horizon oil spill and heavy industry pollution to flocks of birds flying in unison and the trajectory of stars across a clear sky.

The poets did not use a stage but moved about the audience at first clumsily and then more gracefully. As the energy of the room began transforming, the poets not speaking at the moment lovingly placed hand-sewn, detail-rich pillows in the laps of folks. The pillow had been adorned with long, soft pieces of fabric the women then wrapped around each person as an embrace. The final poet initiated a prayer of water and life and peace as the video changed to a gentle creek and the hum of children splashing. All five poets drew together in the center of the room and held hands. The silence shared by the audience and the poets lasted almost five minutes. We'd created and shared a true moment's peace with one another.

Everything Merrill does is working on multiple levels, his studio work feeds his writing which feeds his deep commitment to social activism which feeds his collaborative art which feeds his skill at teaching which feeds his printmaking which feeds his joy of life. He is a dreamer and chaser of visions, as he so well describes himself:

> …My work and approaches to make art have significantly changed, and yet in many ways, they have remained the same. In the past 30 years, I have worked as a community artist, producing complex arts actions both locally and internationally. I have also continued my studio work, including working on sequential etchings each year.
>
> The two seemingly separate modes of creativity, studio art and socially engaged art, feed and provide freedom and validity for each other. These consistent and varied interests in my life as an artist have always led me to return to that "first" etching. The advice provided by teachers and other artists, and the process I have developed over this time still seems new, deeply valid and refreshes my imagination and desire to engage in a continuing dialogue of creative discovery.
>
> Each new generation defines the values of a discipline. When I started my work in 1968, there were two main currents in contemporary art, pop art and abstract expressionism. These two movements strongly influenced the direction a generation of print artists was taking. Always tilting the present conceptual views were artists such as: Peter Milton, Warrington Colescott, Lynne Allen, Ruth Weisberg and June Wayne. All of these people approached print from the depths of their own unique studio narrative.
>
> Today we hear of the Outlaws of printmaking: Tom Huck, Bill Fick, Sean Starwars, Michael Krueger, Jenny Schmid and other rambunctious print artists. To a great degree, printmakers have always followed a different drummer, filling the role of outlaws and expressing their own eccentric visions. Where will that vision go next? What new artist and discoveries will grow out of this magic discipline?

—Jeanette Powers

Beauvais Lyons
Ornithological Quadruped:
Amazonian Lizard Hawk
Lithograph
28" x 22"
2013

photo courtesy of the artist

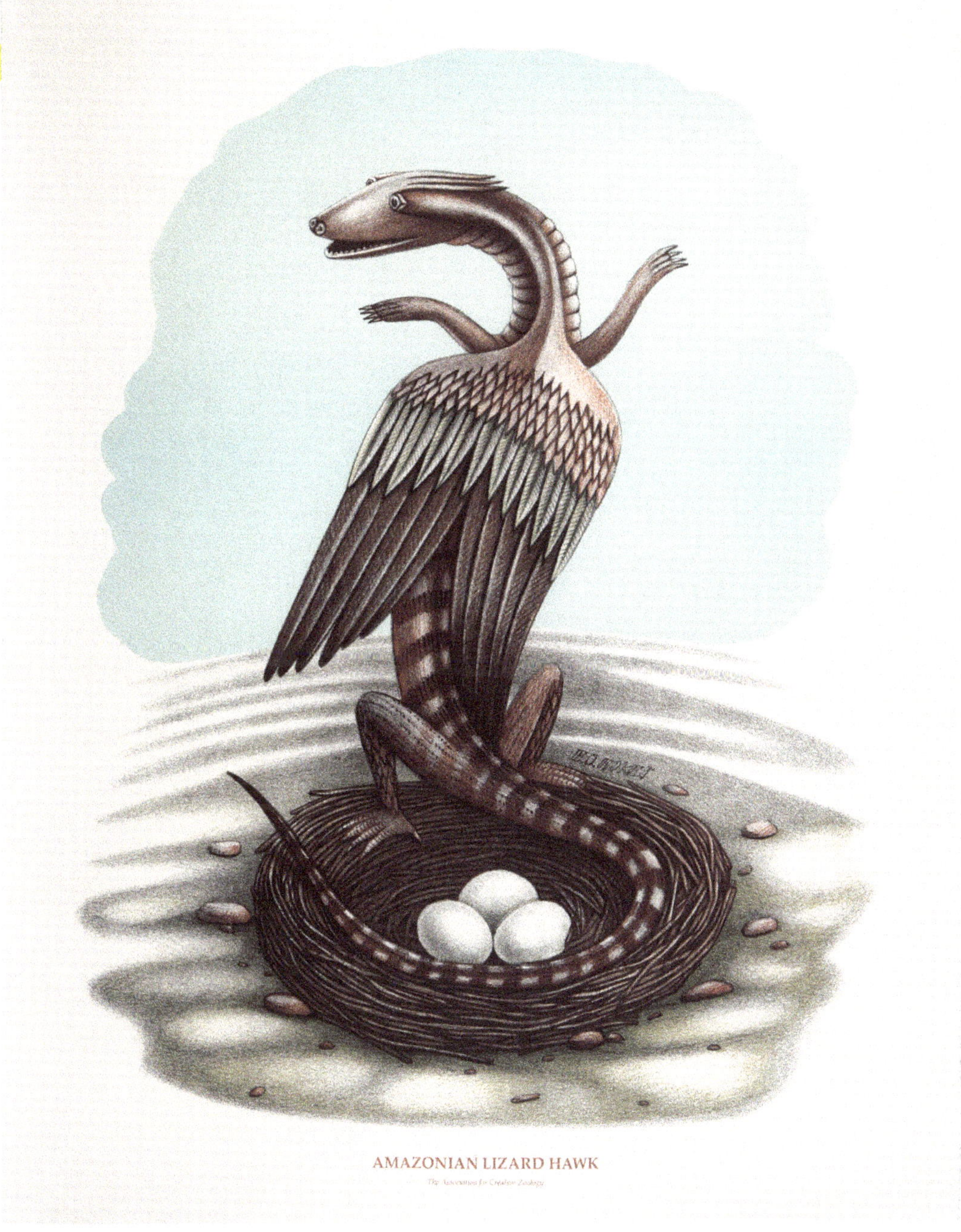

FIRST ETCHING

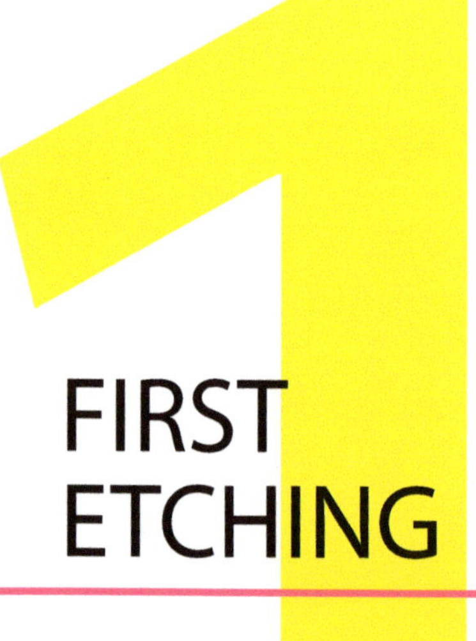

 come from many places. Ways of channeling creative energy arise from a myriad of influences, which vary for every person. Many times, it can be difficult for an artist to determine which way to go to develop an idea. Some ideas seem to emerge completely on their own, almost as if artists were following something outside themselves. Ideas can take on a life of their own and continue beyond the original artist, project, or class. For artists working and discovering their creative paths, others' work and methods can be instrumental in developing a personal methodology, especially in the media of printmaking, which can seem prohibitively technical.

A drawn line will always be simpler to make and understand than an etched line, simply because there is no time delay between the making of the mark and the paper, or another surface, it ends up on. Drawing is a direct process, so nothing is hidden or mysterious. In print, the technical barrier between paper and line can slow the creative process for some. Hugh Merrill found that leaving room for randomness in the creation of work can augment this factor, which can seem detrimental, and turn it into a rich positive.

"It almost killed me," Merrill has been known to comment about his Lucky Dragon suite, which was first exhibited at the Nelson-Atkins Museum of Art, in Kansas City, Missouri, in 1985. The series started as a personal response to a Japanese maritime disaster. A nuclear-bomb test destroyed a fishing vessel, setting off a firestorm of publicity and rage that resulted in a $2 million payoff from the United States to the Japanese government (1). This test was conducted by the United States in 1954 and was specifically designed to provide maximum lethal fallout. At the time, Merrill had been working on atmospheric and structural concepts and imagery, which dovetailed well with the sad fate of the Japanese fisherman.

Merrill produced a new etching daily over several months, resulting in 70 separate pieces. In the process, he weakened the zinc plate until it had no structural integrity and could no longer be printed. Here, Merrill talks a little bit about how he got started drawing and etching and comments on the beginnings of his methods of self-discovery and the role of chance and history that he began exploring as a youth and continues to do so today.

If Only I Could Depend on Growing Old (1969) is from the same time period as Merrill's first etching. In a similar manner, the zinc plate was left in an acid bath for an undetermined amount of time. This technique is an aspect of Merrill's work that continues into the prints he makes today.

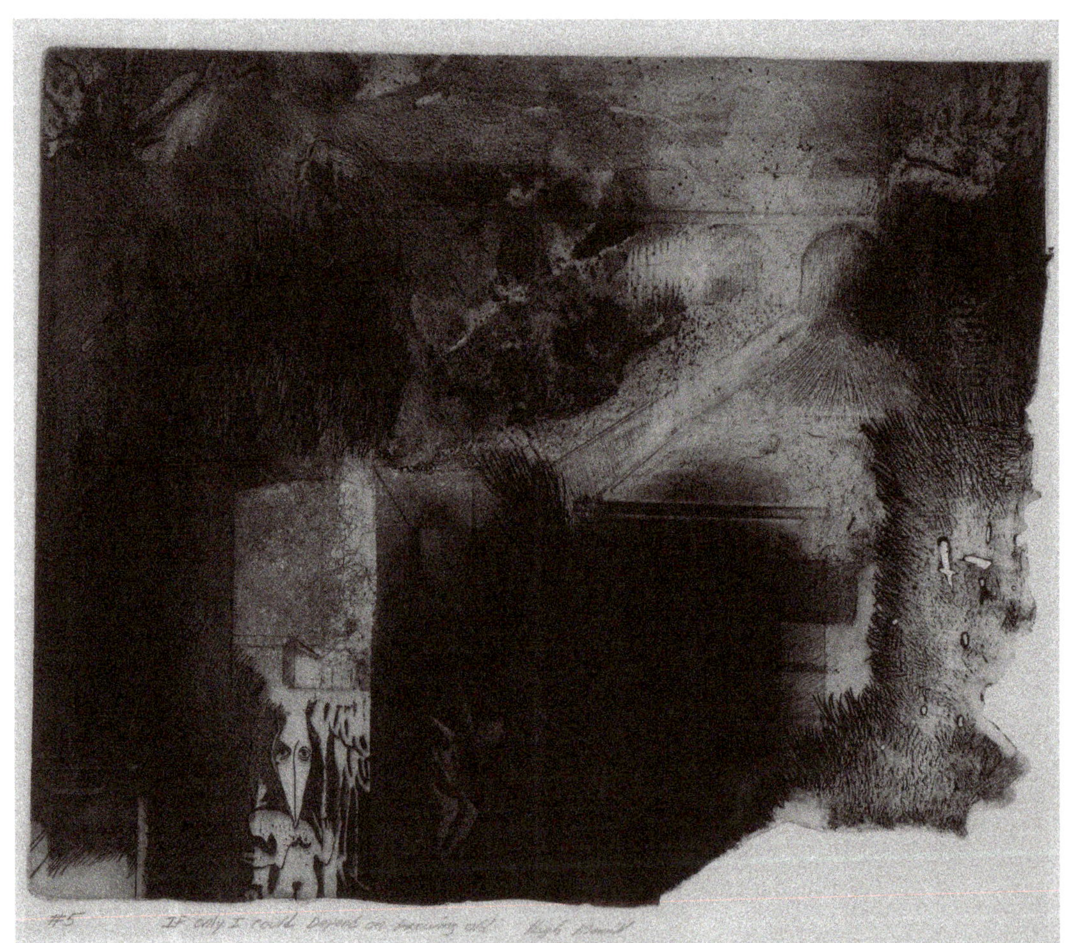

Hugh Merrill
If Only I Could Depend
on Growing Old
Etching
9" x 12"
1969

I was learning to draw in 1968. At that time, we had 12 hours of drawing with a model each week at the Maryland Institute College of Art in Baltimore, Maryland, where I was a student. Each night in my apartment, I would copy the work of Max Beckmann, James Ensor, George Grosz and others. I was drawing abstractly on large sheets of brown paper using a variety of mediums, including paint and charcoal. Photographs and collage materials from newspapers and magazines were then pasted onto the images.

I had found an old cardboard box in the closet of my apartment in the Marlborough building which was filled with black-and-white porn magazines and several years' worth of Disabled American Veteran magazines. All this showed up in the drawings.

The Marlborough had been one of America's most posh apartment buildings back in its day. It housed the Cone sisters, who spent much time in Paris at the movable feast, where they bought Matisse's, Picasso's and Degas's works at very little cost. Their collection would later form the core of the Baltimore Museum of Arts' collection. By 1968, this once-wealthy area was dirt poor. The beautiful, old brownstones lining Eutaw Street had been broken up into small apartments for the diaspora of Southern African Americans moving to the North.

The Marlborough had lost much of its grace but had rooms that testified to past wealth. Apartment had bathtubs that a 6-foot man could easily float in, marble countertops with brass fixtures—all the good stuff. The building was now falling apart and had been taken over by students and artists hanging around MICA. The residents included John Waters and his starlet Divine, who, at the time, were making the now infamous film Pink Flamingos. Artists, students, poets and eccentrics came and went in our own version of the movable feast, but there was a lot more pot in our neighborhood in 1968 than there was in Paris.

In my sophomore year, I took an etching class taught by Peter Hooven. He spent most of the class drinking beer at the bar just down the street. The class started at 9:00 in the morning. If I needed to talk to my teacher, I had to walk down to the Mt. Royal Tavern, which was always worth the walk, because I ended up in an interesting conversation and he bought me a couple of beers in the process.

I began to be drawn toward etching and found that, in printmaking, there was no solid, contemporary current. In painting, students were told what contemporary art was and how to make it. At the time, painting strips or knock-offs of abstract expressionism made up most of the palette.

Print was more obscure and mystical in both history and process. I started by tracing an image from one of the porn magazines I found in the closet onto the plate and then added geometric divisions with a ruler. Like most young artists, I was focused on control. Twelve years in the American public school system had taught me about control and to know the answers to the questions long before they were asked.

Thinking, feeling and creative vision were not part of the curriculum. Just knowing the answer does not mean that it is creative or interesting. Vision and creativity are more than correct answers and come about more slowly through acquired knowledge, life experience, time and experiential interaction. Knowledge grows from contact, participation and reaction to the dialogue of creativity. When I began making drawings and etchings, I was automatically driven toward control, trying to think up the meaning of the work and then illustrate it. Think it up first, and then make it, rather than becoming a part of it from beginning to end.

The print process is a guardian against control for the beginning student, throwing in the artist's way frustration, evil misdirection and a tornado of chancy operations. How many drops of acid do I use for this litho? How long do I leave the plate in the acid for etching and so on?

Let me step back. In the beginning, the etchings I made were drawings on zinc plates, which were etched a single time and printed, oddly coming out in reverse. There was little reason these first etchings should not have simply remained drawings. Yet there was something that drew me to stay with what I saw as an outdated process.

The day came when my zinc etching plate with the tracing of two nudes from a magazine, coupled with a good deal of cross-hatching in the background, was put in the acid for a 20-minute etch. I left the print room and went to the Mt. Royal Tavern. I returned after several beers, a game of pool and much good conversation. The plate had been in a new 6 to 1 acid solution for three hours to my eyes, it was ruined. I left the plate on a table, pissed off but unable as yet to toss it and headed back to the bar.

In the morning, Hooven came in to class prior to going out for a drink. When the class gathered, he held the plate up in front of everyone. It was so deeply etched it was a relief sculpture. Hooven said, "Thank, God, this is an etching!" He asked who did it, and when I raised my hand, he looked unsure and understood it was a mistake, not a defining creative risk.

I took the compliment with acceptance. I needed it, and Hooven asked me to print the plate. I re-filed the edges before printing as they had transformed from perfectly rounded, straight, mirror-finished lines to what could have been the topography of a river bank. I did my best to repair the damage and then inked the plate and began wiping it with a tarlatan. The ink clung to the deep areas with a richness I had never seen before. The cross-hatched areas that had been etched away held a fine, thin skin of ink and were surrounded by a dark, ink halo. The delicate drawing of the figures' faces had etched together to produce a mask, foreground, and background, complicating the reading of the space. I began to feel that I might have something, and when I had completed wiping the plate, I placed it on the press bed.

Hooven had blotted a piece of Arches Buff paper and positioned it. I turned the crank on the press and felt the pressure increase as the plate went under the roller. Hooven pulled the felts back, slung them over the roller, and carefully lifted the paper from the plate. He smiled and said, "Now that's an etching," and flipped the plate onto a table for all to see. I was awestruck; the drawing was greatly improved by the etching process. The simple act of allowing the acid to do the work had changed everything. The attack by the acid had taken a rather trite image and turned it into something much more profound and mystical.

The space described in the print was not easily determined. The richness of the lines was dynamic and the ink achieved a physicality in the black areas I had no idea existed. The straightforward content the nudes possessed was interrupted and placed in a new light, questioning the male gaze and giving power to the nude, feminine figures. I was on my way but not quite sure if the work were mine to possess or just a lucky accident.

It would take years to digest all that went into making this first etching. At first, it seemed easy to just etch the hell out of the plate, but that was not the lesson. The lesson was to allow chance into the process, to move as an artist among control, virtuosity, and openness to new opportunities, content and possibilities.

This recognition was not only skill based and technical but also based in meaning and content. New images that seemed to come from beyond my intellect led me to new interpretations and social investigations of my subconscious imaginings.

Later, while at the Maryland Institute, I would meet John Cage and Allen Ginsberg. Only God knows why they would take an interest in my work, but they did. Cages's concern for leaving space for chance in the studio narrative and creative process had an immense impact on my work as a printmaker. I had been writing poetry in 1970, as well as making prints and large mixed-media drawings.

Emmanuel Navaretta, Cage and Ginsberg came up to my apartment on Baltimore Street near MICA to look at my work. They liked the direction of the prints and drawings, so I got cocky and handed Ginsberg my sketchbook, which I turned to a page of my poetry. He read the poem, gently closed the sketchbook, looked me in the eye, and said one word: "Paint." Navaretta and Cage broke out laughing, and so did I.

I guess I knew the poetry was pretty trite stuff, and the advice given was concise and good humored. Then Cage got serious, and posed this idea for writing or creativity in general. He told me to select four areas I knew a lot about: family, my erotic life, the Civil War and high school. He took a piece of paper off my desk and drew two circles and divided each into quadrants. In the quadrants of one circle, he wrote 1 minute, 5 minutes, 8 minutes and 30 seconds. He wrote the subject areas in the second circle: Civil War, erotic life and so on. He then took dice from his pocket and rolled a single die on the subject and the other on the time circle. He told me to write without thinking about the selected subject for the amount of time the dice directed and to continue the process 10 times. I was to take that text, created by both knowledge and chance and work from it, discovering new ideas and relations based on the chance operation of the dice. Over the next several weeks, I played with the process, making a series of writings. This process and writing in general did not open up for me, but I learned a more important lesson and have applied it to my prints and drawings ever since.

Several years later, in graduate school, William Bailey and Al Held, two very different types of artists, both talked about creating a

THE GAP BETWEEN
WHAT WE THINK
AND WHAT WE
MAKE IS THE AREA
OF DIALOGUE.

dialogue with the image. Their sense of dialogue seemed to mirror Cages's idea of opening the creative process to the operations of chance. The artist provides input and then looks at and lives with the image in the studio, allowing new connections to form.

The image is concrete, and thoughts are illusive and nonmaterial. The gap between what we think and what we make is the area of dialogue. Artists no longer work from a theory, concept, or fantasy/mental imaging of what has to be done. They look at what already is and make decisions based on the material reality of the physical work. This always leads to ideas different than the original conceptual inspiration.

Peter Milton, Evan Summers and many other extraordinary print artists apply their images to the plate by drawing. The etching process, with its incised lines and plate tone, provides the image with a richness and physicality difficult to achieve in drawing alone. For me, the drawing is the first step to enter the plate. My images lie under the plate's pristine, mirrored surface, not on it. Images lie inside the plate and have to be carved out of the metal surface.

I often attempted to draw with the precision of Albrecht Dürer, Milton, or Summers, but for me, the etching needle cutting through the ground was always the first layer, which would eventually be etched, sanded and scraped away to leave only archeological remnants of the first drawing efforts. The images were built up by combining aquatint, soft ground, line etching, engraving, and, most importantly, scraping and grinding the surface away, transforming it into trace memories of previous incarnations. The burnisher, scraper and disc sander I used for grinding the metal surface were as integral to the image as the etching needle.

For eight years, from 1968 to 1976, I created abstract landscape images using this process. When the image reached its final stage, I would then pull small editions of 10 or so prints. Eventually, I began to recognize that each image had more life through sequence and variation. I found that the plate had multiple conclusions and multiple complex narratives. I had always been drawn to Rembrandt's multiple states of The Three Crosses and other plates. I began to produce sequential etching monotypes, pulling one, two, or three prints from each state, rather than an edition. At times, I would create as many as 70 unique prints from a single zinc plate, as I did with the Lucky Dragon suite (1985) and the Tower Series (2012) made at Guanlan Printmaking Base in Shenzhen, China.

Eventually, I began to recognize that each image had more life through sequence and variation.

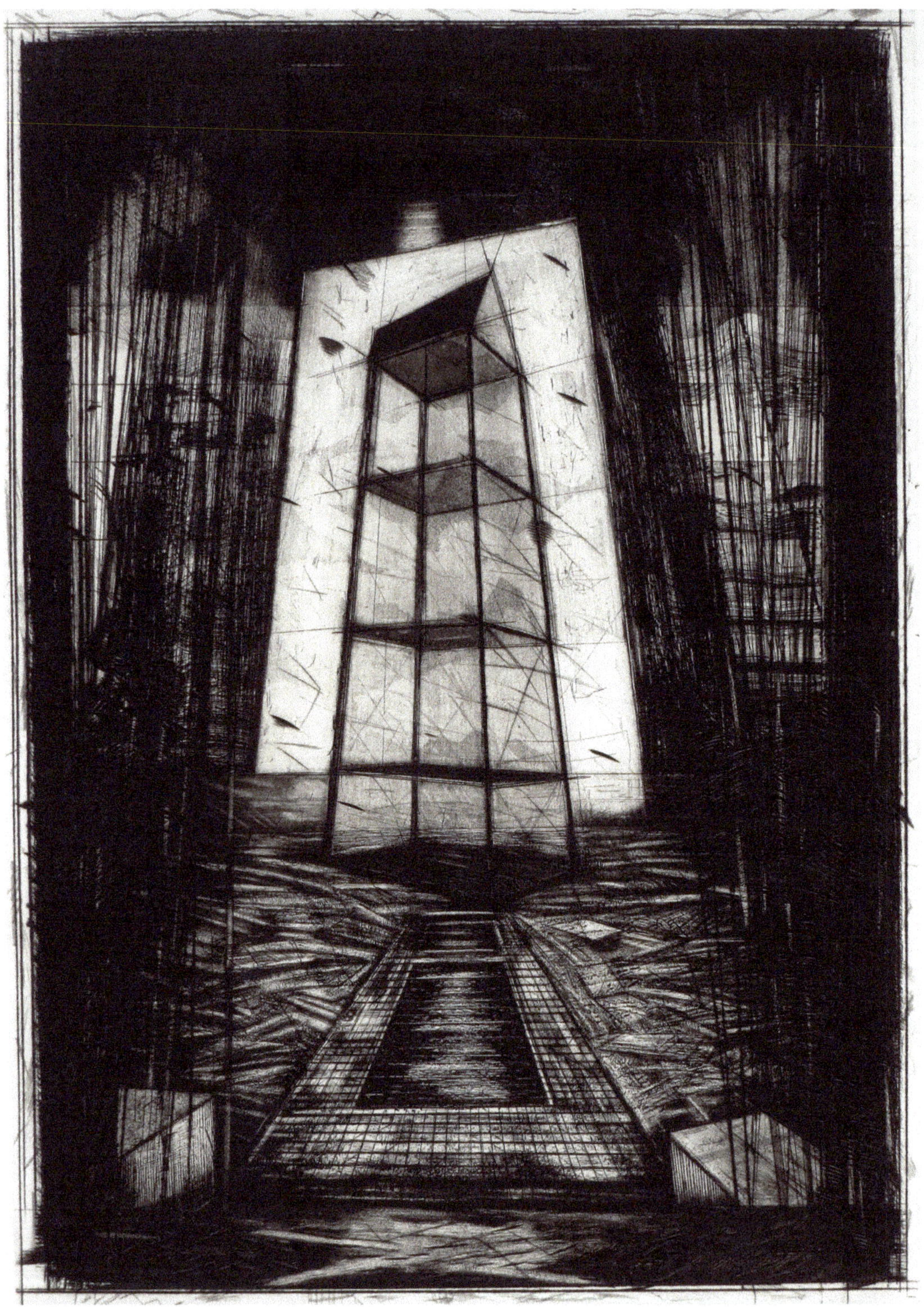

Hugh Merrill
House of
Knowledge: Logic
etching, 24" x 36"
2012
ed. 5

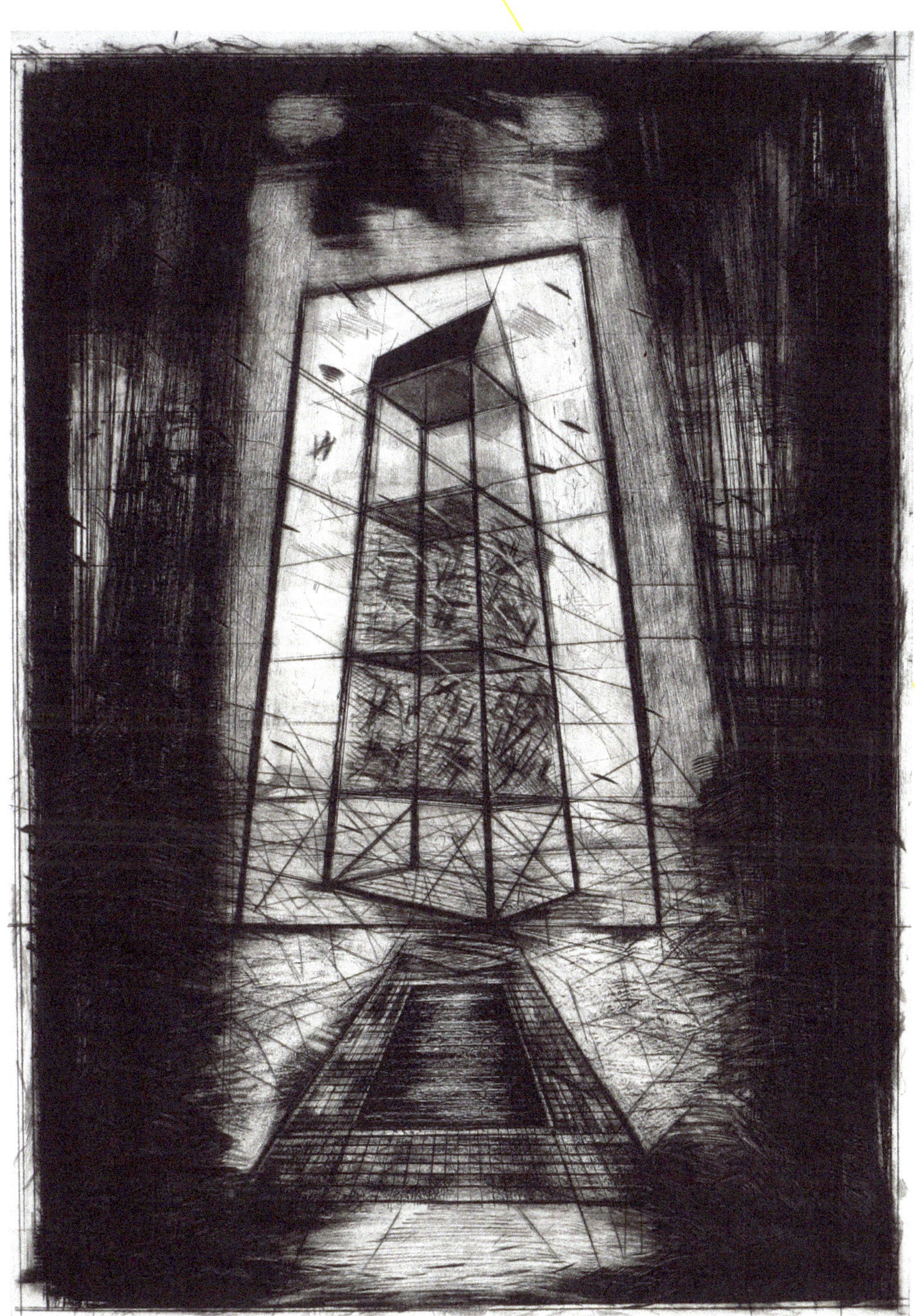

Hugh Merrill
House of Knowledge: 1
Etching
24" x 36"
2012
ed. 5

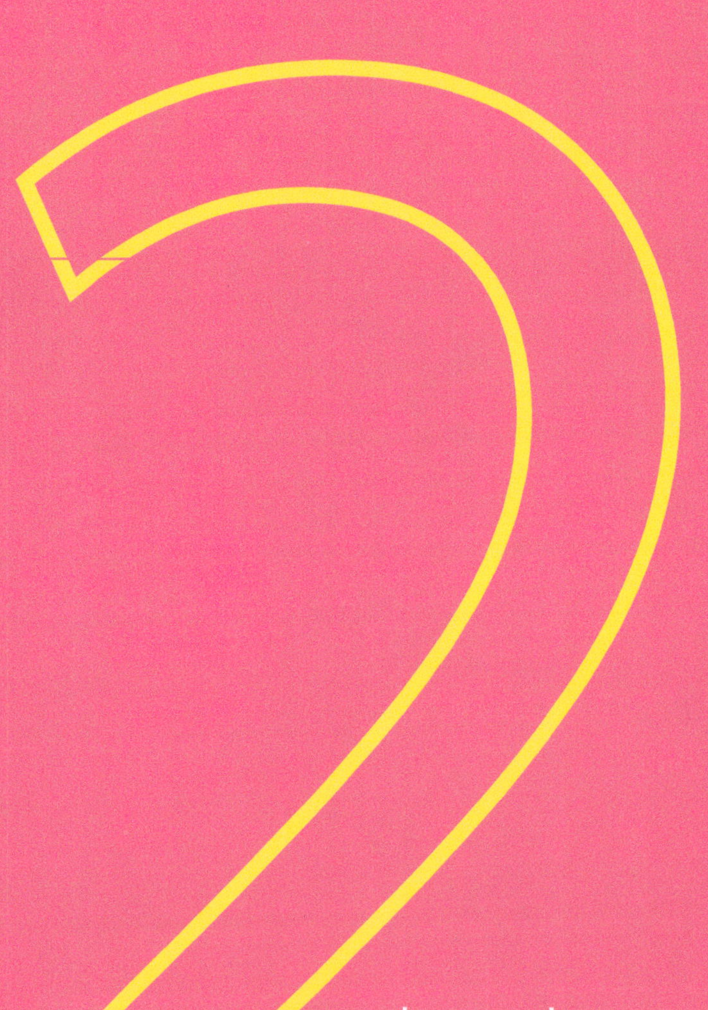
2
beyond
POST PRINT

 Hugh Merrill defines printmaking as an idea, not a set of techniques or processes. Merrill and Steve Murakishi fleshed out and expanded these ideas in the late 1980s.

Murakishi, Merrill and others saw that print would continue to be enriched by its core aesthetic disciplines: lithography, relief printing, screenprinting and etching. Print, at the same time, would expand as a conceptual medium dealing with social subjects—politics, ecology, social issues, and global communication—through multiples, copier art, bumper stickers, offset printed materials, installations and stencils placed on train cars and urban walls.

Print would no longer be defined solely as pressure, ink, and paper, as thoughtfully described by artist and writer Ruth Weisberg. Groups of outlaws, tricksters and revolutionaries began to enter the discipline of print, rearranging and disregarding old rules and structures and turning the aesthetic boundaries from solid fortress walls into porous membranes allowing change, flow and transgression.

Merrill helps explain how these initial thoughts were formed:

> I sat in the basement of Steve Murakishi's house near Cranbrook Academy, where he was the resident artist in the printmaking department. We shot pool, drank a bit, and plotted the ongoing reinvention of print, which we both saw as critical in the limelight of postmodern theory.
>
> The art world had changed significantly, moving from the traditional modernist Greenbergian world of absolutes and purity of form to a wild, rambunctious cacophony. Everywhere there seemed to be the sound of new ideas under construction.

The following year, Steve, Deborah Wye and I would do a presentation at the Southern Graphics Council Conference Tributaries, which was organized by Eleanor Erskine and the Kansas City Art Institute [KCAI]. I went first, starting by reading Post Print: Staking Claim to the Territory, an article I had written. Steve did a hysterical presentation that stated: "Printmaking and painting had been a couple for a very long time. Print had broken it off with paint and had started to date around. It was doing quite well with graphic design, community art and other suitors." I could see the painting faculty from KCAI furrowing their brows, whispering and frowning as Steve spoke, a good sign, indeed.

Wye's discussion at the Southern Graphics Council conference of the exhibition Committed to Print at the Museum of Modern Art (MoMA) in New York in 1988 consisted of many artists who had moved their work onto the streets to communicate with commuters. Barbara Krugers' prints were installed on the walls of construction sites. David Hammon's Free Nelson tags and Alfredo Jaar's subway project Rushes are a few examples. Wye spoke of prints in the streets, posters against the Vietnam War, and artist collectives, including the Guerilla Girls. Her presentation not only mapped out the new territory of printmaking but also established a profound connection to relational aesthetics and community arts practice.

Over the coming decade, more and more artists would take their works and voices to the street: Banksy, Swoon and Sheppard Fairy were a leading wave in what would become social practice. A concern with social justice, rather than the progression of art history and disciplinary aesthetics, came to the forefront. As revolutionaries, tricksters, and outlaws, these artists opened new doors, destroying the old status quo of the cultural time and place. Comparisons can be made with Fluxus of the 1960s, but this movement created not a new cultural "-ism" but something more profound: a creative society in flux.

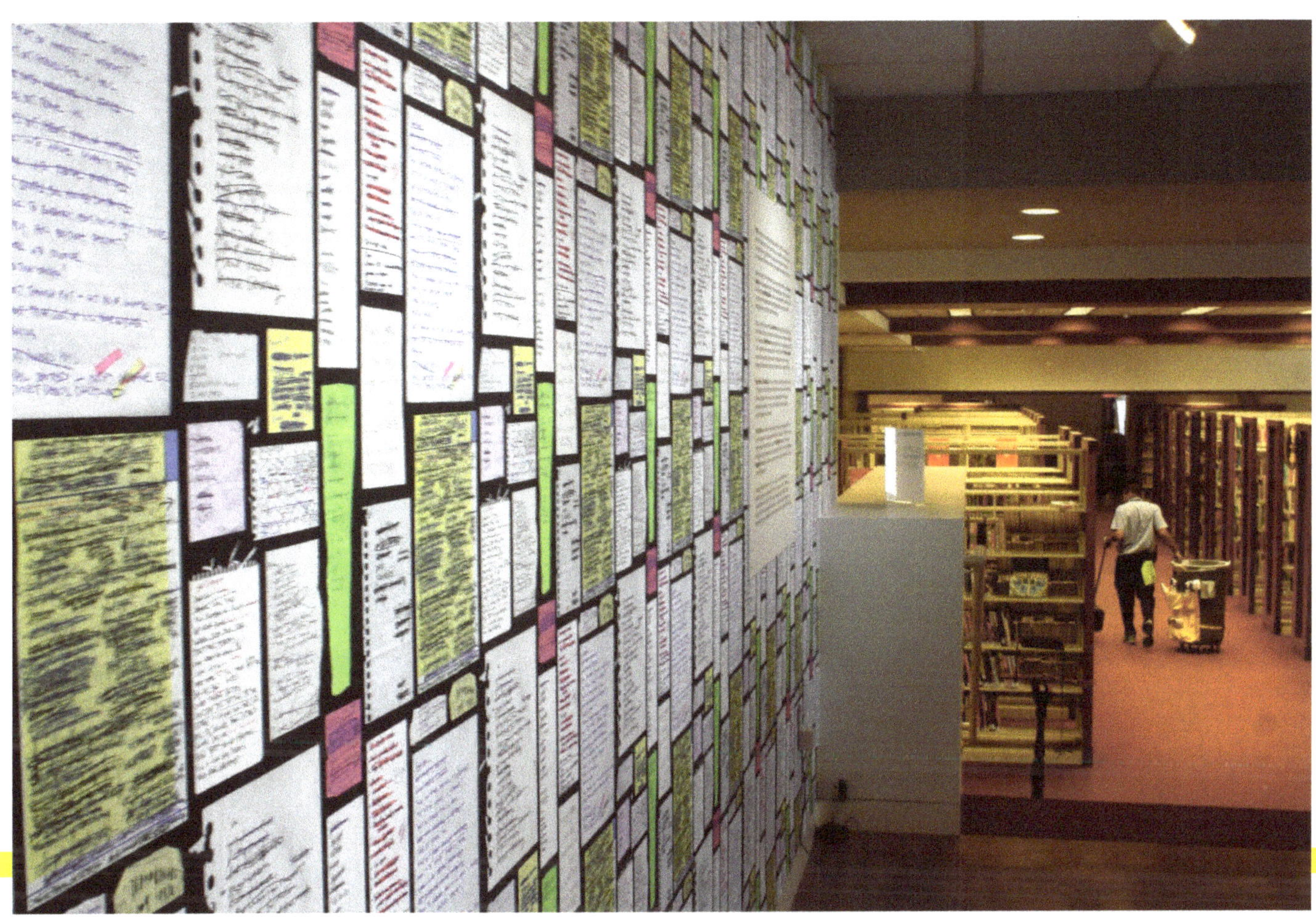

Frances Myers invited Merrill to present Post Print: Staking Claim to the Territory at the panel Printmakers: Quislings of the Art World at the College Art Association in Chicago in 1993. To their surprise, the room filled up quickly the audience spilled down the hallway as a wide variety of artists and curators tried to get into the panel presentation. All the panel's ideas were thoughtful and provocative, moving print forward to capture new creative territory. Merrill was humbled when he was asked for permission to publish Post Print in a number of international and national print periodicals, including Printmaking Today and Contemporary Impressions. Beauvais Lyons of the University of Tennessee included the piece in the print bibliography published at the Southern Graphics Council's Printology conference in Philadelphia. The article also appeared in Lyons' Critical Reading in Printmaking.

To their surprise,
the room filled
up quickly and
the audience
spilled down the
hallway...

STAKING CLAIM TO THE TERRITORY

Over the past two decades, the creative role played by print has shifted from a firm grounding in modernist, painting-based aesthetics to encompass a much broader, undefined territory. Historically, the boundaries defining printmaking have been limited to technical categories, and a print was defined as the map but not the territory described by the map. The function of language in defining printmaking was to act as a signifier, to name phenomena and to break down subjects into technical processes. However, the meaning of language lies not in the definitions of words but in communicating their broader abstract relationships.

Language is not static but evolving. Just as language cannot be defined as an alphabet, words, definitions, or syntax, print cannot be defined as a series of technical activities. It is more appropriately defined by the function, philosophical usage and evolution of the ideas it spawns. Print can stake claim to creative territory that goes beyond any map; the meaning of the images produced through printmaking become the territory defining it.

Until the present, there has existed in print a hierarchy based on technical categories or the means of production which values lithography, etching, screenprint and relief as fine arts. Offset, copier and computer prints are valued as reproductive and commercial ventures. Collaboration opposes the creative effort of the individual print artist, the edition opposes the unique impression, and the copier pamphlet the letter-press volume. Breaking down this hierarchy leads to further analysis according to function.

Viewing print's duality from a modernist position led to an exclusionary definition which prevented print from staking claim to the full extent of its critical and educational possibilities. The modernist ideal of art independent of interpretation, in which meaning has no direct relation-ship to social or topical events, stripped traditional print of one of its essential functions, which is and always has been the communication of ideas. Modernism's search for universality, for a purity of form in which significance resides in the materials and the creative gesture, is alien to print's history of activism and social commentary.

Print artists, including Durer, Groz, Kollwitz, Goya, Baskin, Lasansky and Colescott, have used their unique studio gestures to transform topical events into images of social activism. The history of the medium is the history of artists bridging the distance between private gestures and social commentary.

The continuation of this tradition was well documented in the MoMA exhibition Committed to Print, curated by Wye. She established a relationship between individual gestures and activism, as seen in the works of Luis Cruz Azaceta, Juan Sanchez and Mary Frank. The exhibition also traced an activist role in reproductive processes, including works derived from a lineage of commercialism, posters, Dada and Fluxist publications.

These works communicate directly and publicly beyond the elite institutions of contemporary art. A poster published by the Art Workers Coalition protesting the war in Vietnam asks, "Q. And babies," and answers both visually and linguistically, "A. And babies." The power of this image is a precursor to the works of Sue Coe, Jenny Holzer and Kruger. Here, print acts as a mobile messenger informing an unsuspecting public.

Postmodernism can be more than a vacuous deconstruction of modernism. For print, postmodernism is less a stylistic change than

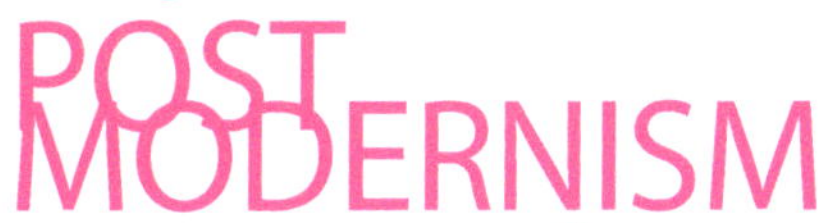

acceptance of the creation of work in relation to a broader community, a function essential to print throughout its history. Postmodernism creates a paradigm in which the duality of print loses its aesthetic significance. The original and the reproductive roles become complementary possibilities, instead of opposing categories.

Print finds itself in an advantageous position. Images produced in creative collaborations between artists and master printers are some of the most effective works in contemporary art. Prints devised in the forms of multiples, installations, new genre and altered photographs have developed a unique aesthetic approach to the issues that concern contemporary visual thought.

Print has contributed significantly to the evolution of twentieth-century aesthetics. The significance of commercial prints is widely recognized: No one, for example, denies that advertisements and billboards have influenced the development of modern and postmodern art. Print lies at the intersection of low and high art, creating images that speak with the clarity of language and the power of entertainment.

Print's direct democratic life focused on communication creates the staggering wealth of images that has accumulated to form the printed landscape in which we live. Through distribution, these images have become the common source of our communal worldview.

A mechanism of diffusion parodies fine-arts elitism as print provides the means to bypass the economic and critical hierarchy of the gallery–museum nexus and go beyond the private language of artists to speak to a broad audience and to function in daily life. Print allows artists to cross the boundaries between art and life, aggressively seeking new audiences. Outside the museum walls, print serves as a mechanism to produce multiples that reach into the community. In this way, print functions as a democratic, direct, modest means of communication, breaking down the function of art as a capitalist object.

Works produced by co-ops which oppose racism and gentrification and explore topics, such as AIDS, gay rights, and the commercialization of art, act as a visual conscience for a broader community. Here, art is created for a specific purpose and breaks the connection with the contemplative function based on painting aesthetics.

These attributes take print beyond a narrow categorical definition, allowing it to claim processes, images and ideas and fulfill creative educational roles. Print can become an arena combining the gestural physicality of craft-making with the new technologies offered by computers, photography, design and mass reproduction. In print, the intersection of direct and indirect creative processes, coupled with a history of activism, creates content reflected in daily political and social struggles. This content provides a significant basis for investigations and the education of the next generation of artists. Achieving balance between spontaneity and the dictates of craft is difficult.

Here lies the critical separation between the painter and the print artist. The same issues are available to both, as is the immediacy of drawing. The print process, though, takes the idea and the artist beyond the confines of the studio gesture, creating not an object for the wall but communication with the world.

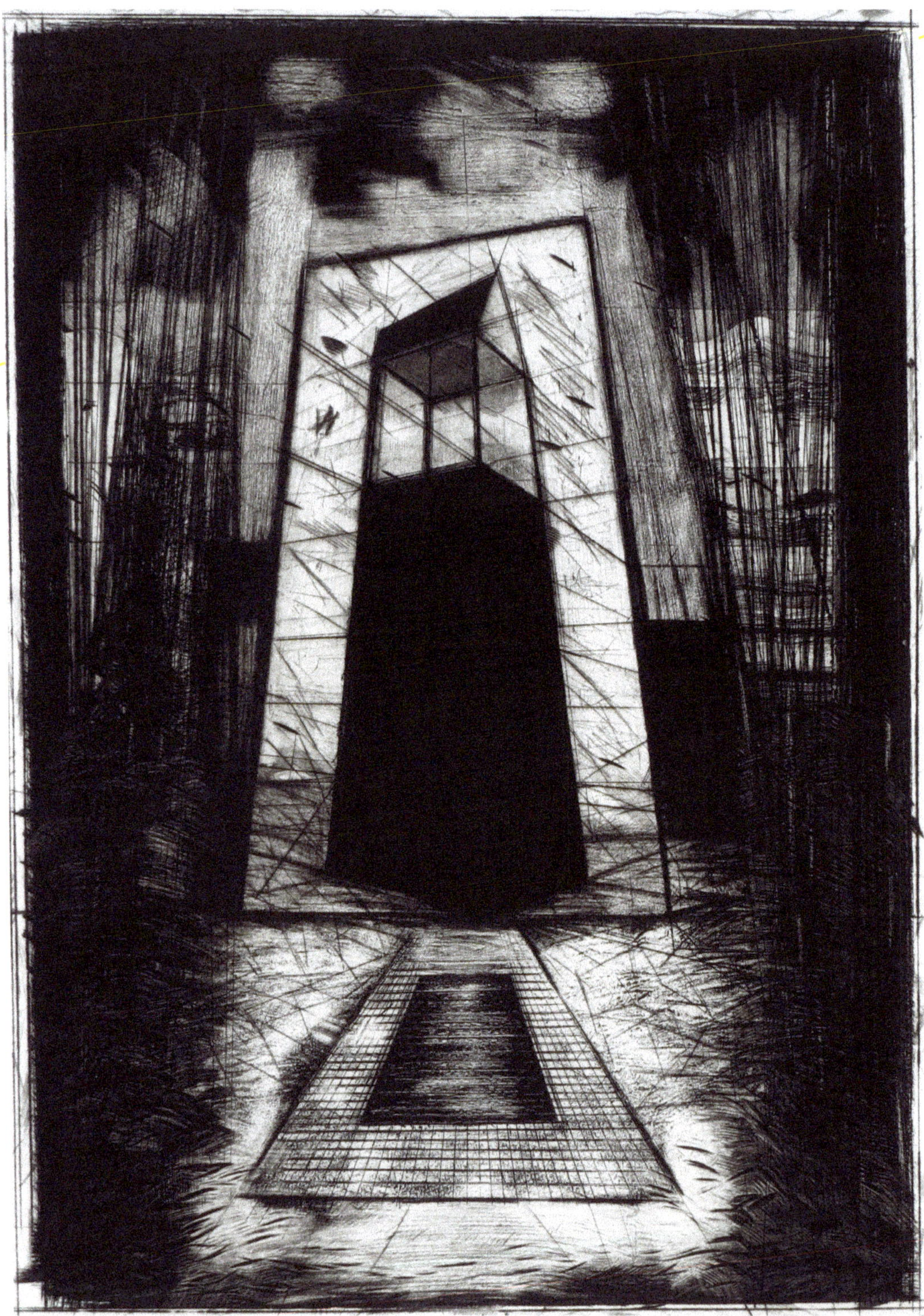

Hugh Merrill
House of Knowledge:
Materialism
Etching
24" x 36"
2012
ed. 7

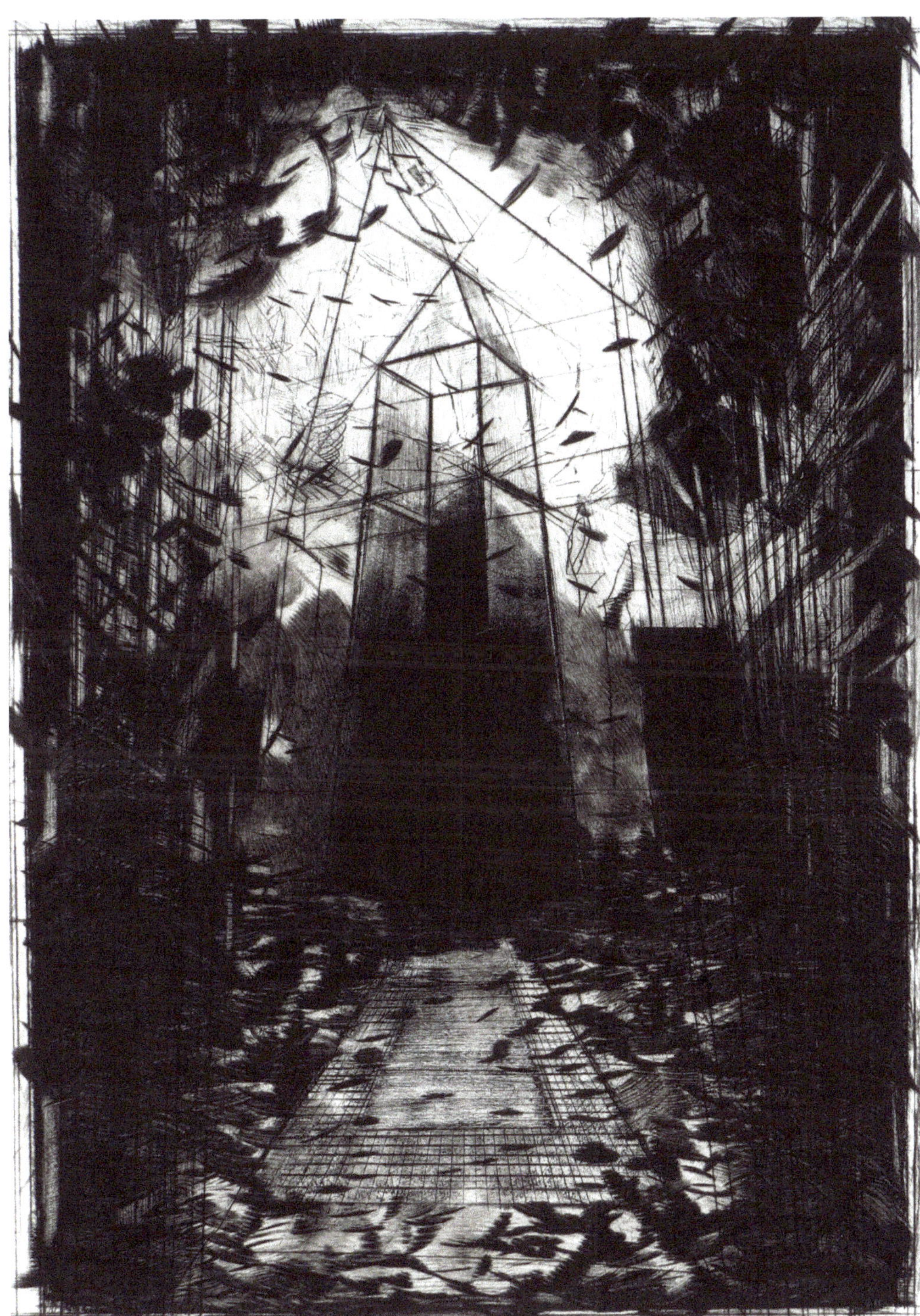

Hugh Merrill
House of Knowledge:
Emptiness
Etching
24″ x 36″
2012
ed. 7

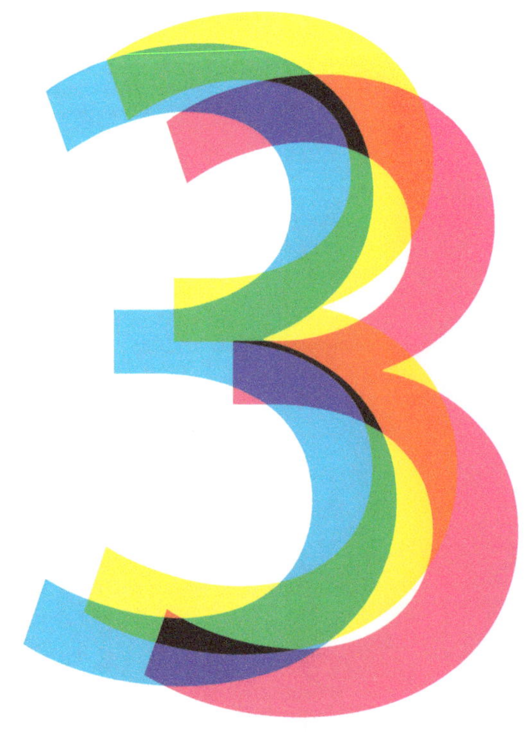

EDUCATING THE NEXT GENERATION *of printmakers*

was written in April of 1991 and as I reread it, I find that a good amount of what was written then is still true today. Since 1991, the growth of social practice, what we called community art back then, has taken on more prominence and is a major interest of the art community and students today. Today, working collaboratively means much more than forming a relationship between a master printer and an artist.

The digital world of communication and production has made mind-blowing changes in the way art is conceived, disseminated and produced. In 1991, no one could have imagined the complexities of social media as we use it today. Photoshop allows anyone to make complex, layered works that are seamless, replacing the high craft and skills of photomontage. Now, the 'darkroom' is in the computer, rather than behind a circular, rotating door leading into a dim room with red lights.

Much has changed, but the overall idea that print curriculum should embrace the broadest disciplinary definition still rings true as we are educating both printmakers and contemporary artists who often do not fit a traditional discipline. Additionally, there should not be a single avenue of education for the printmaker; there should be many. University programs have different institutional structures than art colleges, and community colleges are not like either one. The structural hierarchy within each institution creates a distinctly different environment than learning print in a community print studio, like Saltgrass Studio in Salt Lake City, Utah, or Evil Prints in St. Louis,

Missouri. Each contributes to the richness of the educational diversity of the discipline.

I hope that these thoughts are broad enough to allow for a discussion of all the points of departure for learning printmaking. It is important to allow for the flow of creativity among the creative edge, the core process and historical tradition. This is the realm and dialogue in all crafts, the conversation between the edge and the center.

The versa laser, CNC router, and the 3D printer are amazingly precise tools, providing new opportunities for print-based artworks and concepts, but they will never replace the hand and mind of Tom Huck. Peter Milton is an artist whose craft is in the core process of etching. Milton is unmatched in the media, yet today, he makes digital images with over 100 layers of information.

—Hugh Merrill, June 2016

KNOWLEDGE AND INSTRUCTION

Knowledge and instruction are two different components of the educational process. Instruction is training and learning how-to in the form of skills development, a process of thinking which leads to discovery. It is not an imposed structure but varies with the individual. The end product of knowledge is a self-critical, exploratory and engaged intellect. It is not oriented to goals or seeking an academic payoff like a grade. Instruction is dedicated to learning how to etch a stone or create the softest watery tones on an etching plate with a spit bite aquatint. As artist, educator and designer Ditmar Winkler once said, "Knowledge is for the unknown; training is for the known." The two forms are complements, threaded together to complete any valuable educational process.

Teaching printmaking consists of constantly swinging between these two forms, increasing knowledge while teaching specific skills. "You learn technique so that you do not have to think about how to do something," was a favorite statement by printmaking professor Gabor Peterdi. He repeated this phrase many times while working with students at Yale University in the 1970s. It was his belief that, once you know any given technique deeply, it becomes automatic and intuitive. A good educational process is never a matter of separating the conceptual from the physical or the technical from the poetic but of learning to allow both their place in the creative process.

AN EXPANDING TERRITORY

The printmaking student is situated in one of the best educational departments for becoming a contemporary artist or designer. Over the past three decades, printmaking has grown from its core processes, defined by artist and theorist Ruth Weisberg as the relation between ink, pressure, and paper, to a broader interdisciplinary territory which encompasses much of postmodern artistic practice. Print has expanded from focusing on lithography, etching, relief and screen-printing to include installations and digital productions in all their amazing and diverse forms. Community-based arts actions, Fluxus, new genre public art, events and performances are also included. Printmaking is no longer known solely as artwork derived from the core technical processes because it is a language of evolving ideas.

Print artists present interactive dialogues through offset and copier booklets, posters, pamphlets, underground newspapers and zines. Relational and socially engaged art functions on a new collaborative level, giving political voices to artist co-ops and social justice groups.

Print includes all forms of popular culture: texts, books, information and the documentation of arts or community actions. Each method of production/expression cited offers a unique, vital creative opportunity involving a series of evolving ideas and lines of thought rooted in various histories. Conceptually, print is one of the keys to the interdisciplinary creative process.

Print also enters the world through images produced by collaboration between master printers and artists. These works have become some of the most effective and lasting works in contemporary art. Print involves the intense introspection of the individual etcher, lithographer, silkscreen, or relief print artist. Here, printmakers are also supported and inspired by an international community: artists, curators, exhibitions, exchange portfolios, studios and biennials.

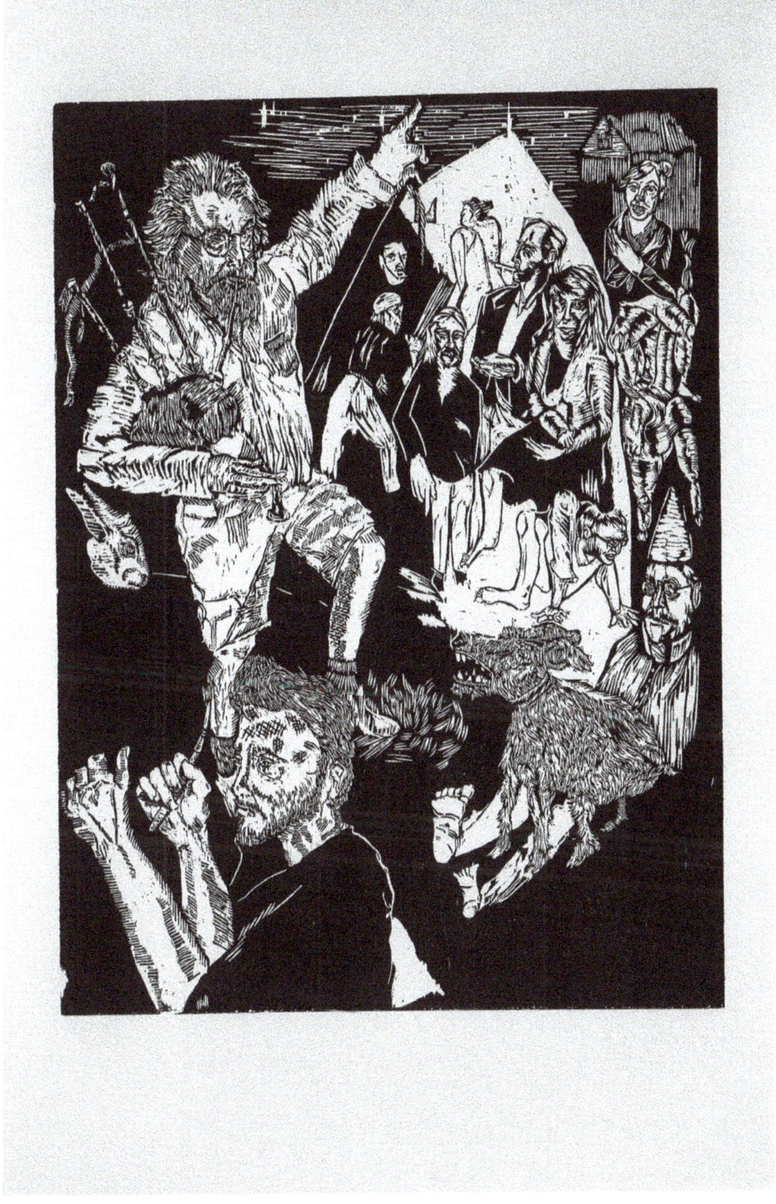

Emmett Merrill
Ballad for Bill McKim
Relief
30" x 44"
2013

photo courtesy of the artist

In the past, printmaking has taken a categorical approach. In education, programs have been built around technical divisions. To address the broad concerns arising from the expansive territory that now defines print, breaking up technical categories into conceptually oriented modules reinforces the standard curriculum. Education structures based on learning individual technologies are, by their orientation, too narrow to explore a broader language in visual culture.

The over-emphasis on technical exploration and achievement can cut the cord binding issues of content with the activity of making. High degrees of craft and aesthetic tradition are important for students. Is it possible to teach both simultaneously? Can we sustain the core and push the boundaries to allow new critical possibilities at the same time, in the same space?

CAN WE SUSTAIN THE CORE AND PUSH THE BOUNDARIES TO ALLOW NEW CRITICAL POSSIBILITIES

AT THE SAME TIME,

IN THE SAME SPACE?

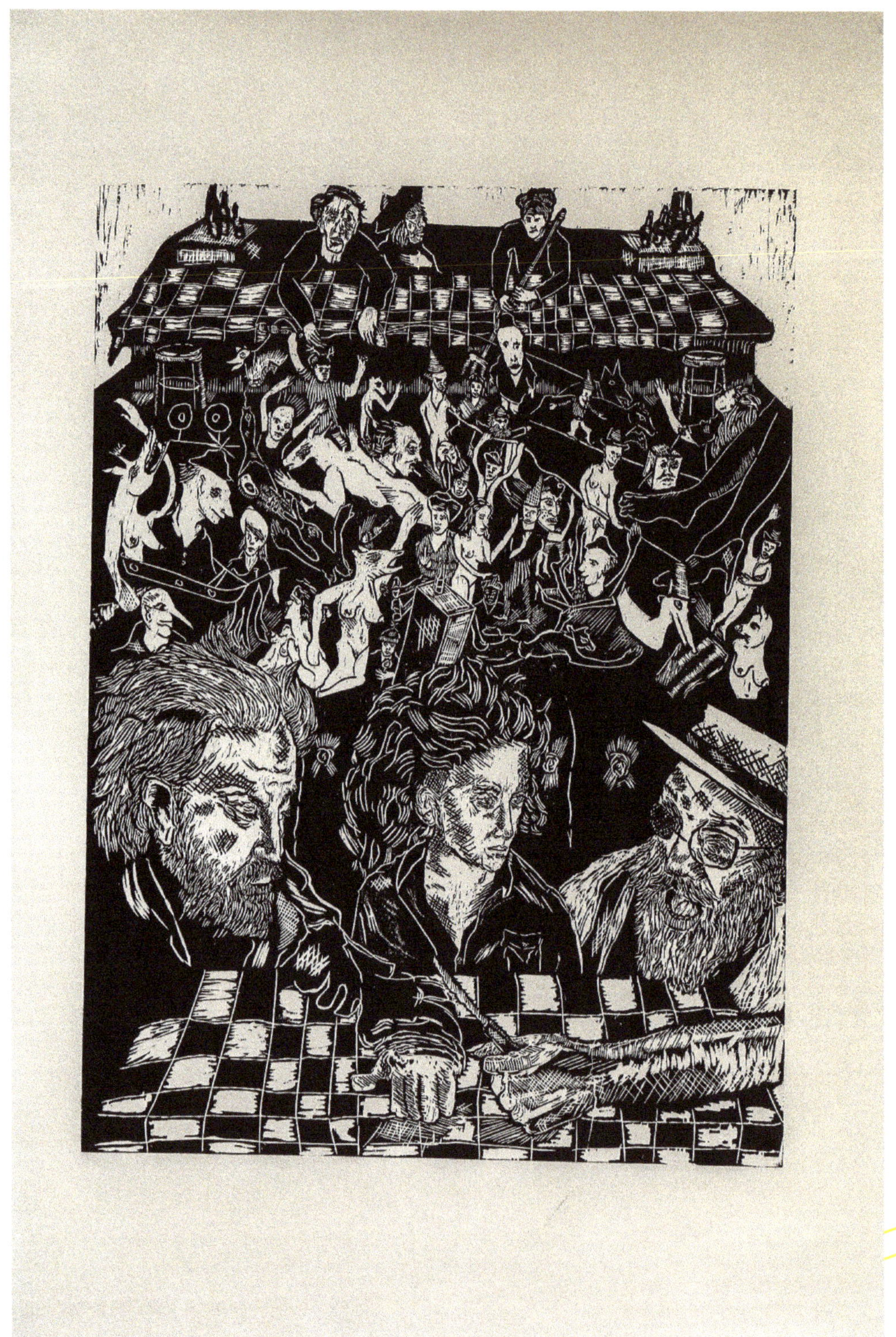

photo courtesy of the artist

Emmett Merrill
A Night at Tender Creek
Relief
30" x 44"
2013

AN ATTEMPT

For the past three decades, the curricular structure at the Kansas City Art Institute (KCAI) has been determined by its programmatic philosophy, validating the investigation of print as a broad interdisciplinary area. This philosophy has resulted in a curriculum that encompasses print's conceptual possibilities and core traditional processes. In the undergraduate program, we balance these processes with interdisciplinary and conceptual investigations.

A highly crafted etching has no more importance than a community-arts interaction helping inner-city and at-risk teenagers publish a zine. Both fall under the rubric of printmaking, yet the two cannot be compared. Each has a different critical and evaluation zone of reference. Each is valid within its own context and is validated within the broader international contemporary print community.

KCAI has developed courses rooted in etching, lithography, relief, and screen-printing and courses that open the discipline to conceptual investigation. Advanced printmaking for juniors and seniors is not focused on a specific technical area but, instead, allows students to develop and follow their own creative journeys, supported by courses that are thematic and discursive in nature.

Classes, such as zines and multiples, dimensional print and installation, and public speaking, help students explore possibilities. Political posturing provides conceptual formats to investigate issues extending beyond a single discipline. For over three decades, we have taught concepts in community art, working to provide students with the opportunity to move from sole authors of their work to facilitators of community arts actions.

Chameleon Arts Caravan is an ongoing exploration of relational aesthetic theory that has worked with adjudicated youth, residents of inner-city geriatric centers, the homeless, domestic-violence-center residents, urban Native Americans, and communities of location, such as coffee shops and bus stops. Most often but not always, the outcomes are based in printmaking. Here, creativity is informed by real-world experience.

THE IMPORTANCE OF AN INDIVIDUAL STUDIO NARRATIVE

The core curriculum encourages a deep studio investigation based on producing work. In the classroom, the print is established as a vital means of expression rather than as a secondary act of reproduction based on forms previously discovered in other mediums. A goal in the curriculum is to have students achieve original, authentic action through the processes of printmaking. It is important for students to develop the fluidity to encounter the material in a physical way and to acquire the sensitivity to manipulate the process to capture their ideas and thoughts for documentation. The studio narrative is a dialogue with a process and ideas leading to new works and insights. In advanced classes, print majors often find that the physical act of making and remaking the image through this process integrates thinking, feeling and translating into artistic expression. It is through the evolution and development of individuals' studio narrative that they begin to determine their level of technical exploration through their choice of medium, conceptual territory and degree of virtuosity achieved.

A successful print can be a simple gesture drawn on an etching plate or a complex combination of photographic or digital investigations that brings together multiple print processes. The print can be a zine, copier poster, or published book on a community arts action. This educational structure allows students to define their own course as they flow through a variety of processes and conceptual territories. The degree of craft and content is determined by individuals' inclination and the logic of their studio narrative. This approach keeps the critical dialogue focused on a balance of process and content issues. Students learn to balance craft with communication and seek to find the correct relation needed in their projects or works.

THE STUDIO NARRATIVE IS A DIALOGUE WITH A PROCESS AND IDEAS LEADING TO NEW WORKS AND INSIGHTS.

What of digital possibilities? The digital is integrated as an important component in each class and is a focal point of the junior year at the Kansas City Art Institute (KCAI). The overall goal is to create flow between the artist's hand and digital media. Many projects ask students to move back and forth seamlessly between two modes of creative thinking. A sketchbook page or drawing might be scanned into a computer, altered in Photoshop, and then transferred to an etching plate, where it is reworked and scanned for further investigation. The two streams move along together, the development of the etching and the similar image in Photoshop. As in much of the work of Dieter Roth, variation and creativity are the content. The inherent delay between gesture and process and the potentially evolving matrix create a series of changing images as printmaking is the territory of possibility and opportunity.

The single skin of the canvas leads to a single, final conclusion. How do we keep a work or idea living and moving toward new or multiple conclusions? Print is a bastion of variation and creativity as content, blessed with near infinite variations. Print is about sequential growth, as seen in the works of artists as diverse as Milton and Roth. The matrix is a memory surface.

This practice is far from an attack on technology or craft. Our programmatic philosophy seeks to keep the student involved in making prints proportional, integrated, and in the end, self-directed. KCAI students have developed an array of interests as broad as the discipline itself. Some have become master printers, such as David Jones, founder of Anchor Graphics in Chicago. Graduates have printed for Landfall Press, Universal Limited Art Editions, Graphic Studios and others.

Students are encouraged to learn and use print so as to fulfill its collaborative aesthetic possibilities. Some students approach print from a vastly different method. They produce copier books, using stamps, drawing on napkins from coffee shops and altering commercially printed images. They give up the traditional processes in search of interdisciplinary modes of communication. Their works often derive from the study of semiotics and have a conceptual orientation. A strong core of students always focuses on expressing their ideas through deep, intuitive knowledge of etching or other traditional core processes. Each approach is respected and offers the others broader possibilities through cross-pollination.

AESTHETIC POSSIBILITIES

In 1968, around the height of abstract expressionism's influence on education, anything that got in the way of direct gesture and interaction with material was considered a negative at the Maryland Institute College of Art. In general, the multi-layered technical processes of print and ceramics were viewed as interference in the intuitive and gestural creative process. Robert Motherwell was the youngest of the New York School of painting, which included Jackson Pollock, Willem DeKooning, Mark Rothko and others. In his work, he combined expressive gesture, automatism and color field work. He has said that "Drawing was the crack of a whip." He advised young artists to be careful when working in print because it has a built-in delay. Printmakers cannot progress beyond drawing until they learn to manipulate this delay, which is the transition from the gesture of drawing to the mechanical processes of the discipline.

Collaborative printing is based around the delay. It seizes the moment when the printer takes over, moving the artist's gesture into another medium. The print artist and student accept and manipulate the delay and make it a continuation of the creative process, rich with possibilities. Here lies the critical difference in the attitudes of the painter and the print artist. Both have available the same resources, as well as the act of drawing. The delay in the act of processing an etching plate is, to one student, annoyingly technical and, to the other, the continuation of creative possibility. To establish a productive, creative classroom attitude is to achieve a sense of fluidity and the ability to creatively manipulate the delay inherent in all print processes.

"TO ESTABLISH A PRODUCTIVE, CREATIVE CLASSROOM ATTITUDE IS TO ACHIEVE A SENSE OF FLUIDITY AND THE ABILITY TO CREATIVELY MANIPULATE THE DELAY INHERENT IN ALL PRINT PROCESSES.

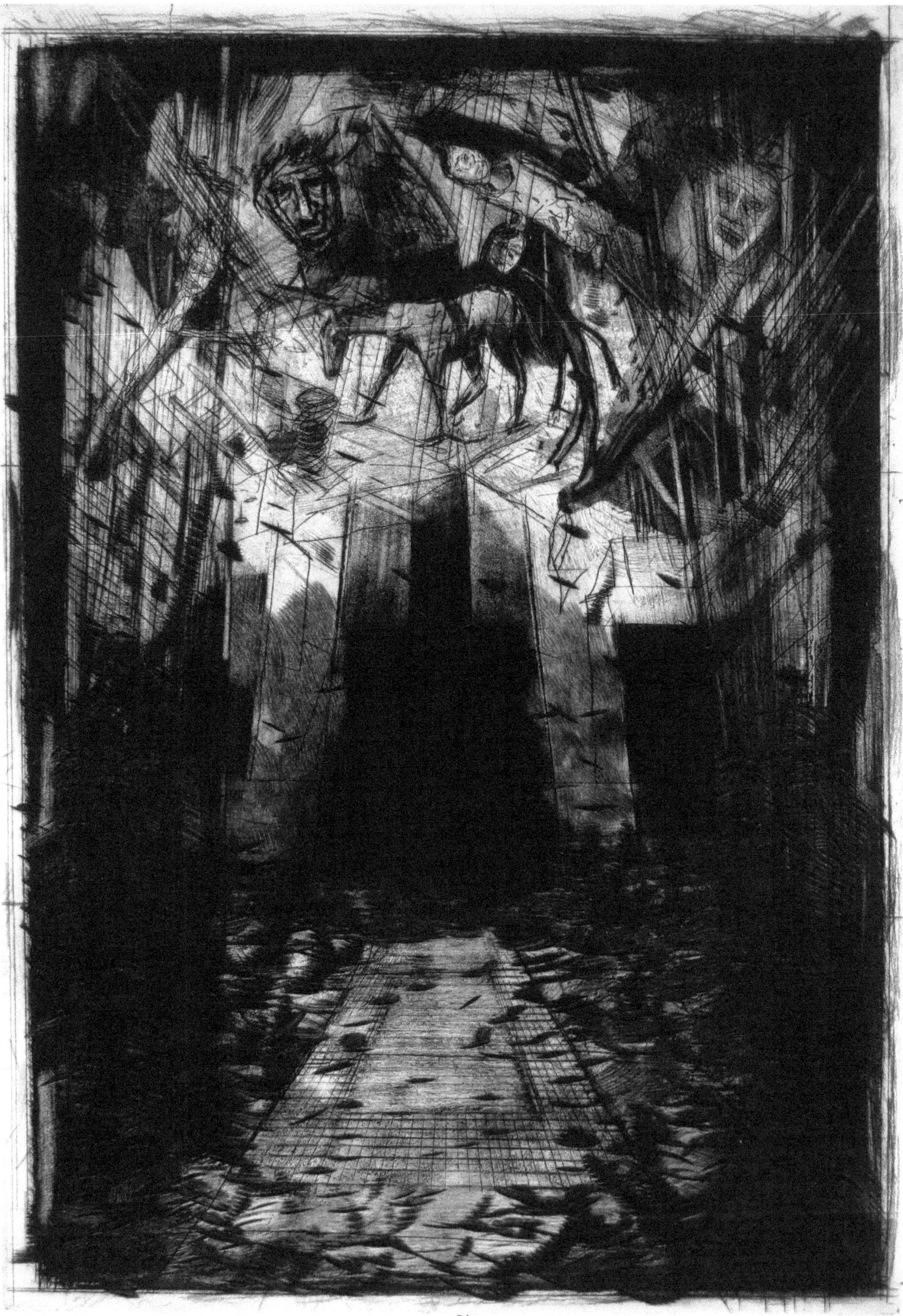

Hugh Merrill
House of Knowledge:
Conciousness
Etching
24″ x 36″
2012
ed. 7

House of Knowledge is a series of etchings made at Guanlan Printmaking Base in Shenzhen, China, in 2012. Over the course of five weeks, Merrill revisited techniques he has used frequently throughout his explorations of the etching media, know as reductive (or suicide) sequential etching.

The structure depicted is a watchtower, a spiritual space that allows one to see the future due to their location in the top of a very tall tower. The piece is presented in a classic worm's eye view, challenging the viewer to determine their own place in Merrill's environmental, conceptual and metaphysical constructs.

4

WHAT IS A QUISLING?
existing in the margins

A QUISLING IS a person who collaborates with an enemy force. The term originates from the Norwegian army officer Vidkun Quisling, who began his career as a military attaché. He encouraged Germany to invade Norway in 1940 and after the war was executed for treason and other crimes. (1)

Artist and educator Frances Myers, then at the University of Wisconsin, Madison, organized the panel Are Printmakers the Quislings of The Art World? at the 1993 College Art Association Conference in Seattle, Washington.

Myers was concerned that a disciplinary system focused on craft (printmaking) to educate young artists would make them feel they were being left behind. She was concerned that young artists might view the title of printmaker as something that would hamper them from achieving critical and career success. Myers also questioned why so many students educated in printmaking denied their background as printmakers. Had they, in fact, become quislings? Were they turning their backs on the experiences that had helped those who came before them to find their voices?

In the case of printmaking, many artists and/or students do drop the title of printmaker. These artists find the word either too narrow to describe the direction of their work, or that the preconceptions of teachers, gallery owners, writers, etc., hamper their careers by placing them in an arts ghetto, where they feel separated from mainstream creative concerns.

Painters and sculptors are seen as inhabiting a wider area, which is less technical and more responsive to the broader theoretical dialogue of contemporary art. Yet an education in painting in no way assures success as an artist, especially for the few who make it to the cutting edge of visual culture. I raise this defensive position because I know that many print students are confronted with a mythical untruth that being in painting is more advantageous. In reality, it is simply difficult to navigate a career as a fine artist, no matter what the area of creativity.

In the disciplines of sculpture and painting, there are many, many more students and individuals participating in educational programs than in printmaking or ceramics, assuring that the per-capita failure rate of sustaining a career as a visual artist is higher than in print or the other craft-related disciplines. The sheer numbers and the difficulty of maintaining a career mean that more painters fail per capita than any other discipline.

Choosing to work in one medium or another should not be based on supposed career opportunities, but on the passion and insight of the individual artist. Different doors open at different times for each artist. The decision to change one's title is most often based on where a person's work and ideas take them, not career issues.

Young artists are looking for an avenue of freedom that does not classify them by medium and process. It may be best for all artists to first call themselves artists and then let their work, ideas and relationships further determine their categorization. In other words, drop the notion of establishing a hierarchy that is both false and detrimental. Looking down on the efforts of another artist never makes a person's own work any better.

Painting is no longer the cutting edge of visual, artistic and creative culture. Contemporary art has moved on to new cross-disciplinary territories that are not discipline based. While working on an exhibition at the Nelson-Atkins Museum of Art in in Kansas City, Missouri, Robert Storr, past curator of painting at the Museum of Modern Art and Dean of the Yale School of Art and Architecture in New Haven, Connecticut, remarked, "Painting should do what painting does best. It should not try to be overly theoretical, conceptual, graphic, or cutting edge. The role of painting is to extend ideas and images into the future through the individual love of the medium and its history."

This sounds a lot like the position that printmaking, ceramic other artistic disciplines have been occupying for decades. In fact, "crafts," which now include painting, should preach to the choir first and allow individuals to push from the center out of their disciplines to discover new areas and ideas. Artists should expand, enrich and even leave their disciplines behind. Artists are like Lewis Hyde's trickster: mythical spirits existing at the crossroads, tripping people up and helping them break out of restrictive situations bound by rules and concrete beliefs. (2)

Young artists are looking for an avenue of freedom that does not classify them by medium and process.

The aesthetic reality of crafts takes the form of a discussion between the center core of aesthetics and the edge that pushes the boundaries of the very definition of the discipline. In print, the aesthetics that have grown for centuries to establish the criteria for a good etching are challenged by the intrusion of books upon Xerox machines and zines that began flitting along the edge of the print community in the 1960s. Artists that worked with Fluxus-and-Dada-related ideas entered print and created an indeterminate space that, over time, has expanded the territory and become a part of the discipline.

Today, all media, from fiber to ceramics, or glass to print, investigate cross-disciplinary postmodern processes and social practice interventions. Many times, artists who start in printmaking, ceramics, fiber, or other traditional art media push beyond the borders of individual discipline by developing alternative paths.

Kara Walker started out making etchings and prints. As she moved into graduate studies, she began to focus on the graphic silhouettes for which she is known. Jeff Koontz moved from painting at the Maryland Institute College of Art in the 1970s to working as a stockbroker in New York before creating a blowup balloon rabbit made from highly reflective metal. He now has an arts fabrication studio with over 100 workers to produce his varied pieces.

Jim Leedy, a ceramist, painter, printmaker, and socially engaged artist, is another example. Leedy first gained recognition as one of the first ceramists to wed clay and abstract expressionism, but he did not let this pin him down. Soon he was creating air sculptures made from parachute silk hanging between 20-story buildings in downtown Kansas

City. Photographs of the flowing sculptures became silkscreens and soon he was off to new territory again. As a socially concerned artist, he helped to turn a mostly abandoned area of Kansas City into the Crossroads Arts District, leading to over a billion dollars in new investments. If artists who make up the cutting edge can matriculate from any discipline, no single discipline has a monopoly on the production of cutting-edge artists. All roads of creativity are valid and productive and have the potential to produce art stars, or lesser-known, highly committed, successful artists.

Crafts, with their strong communities and direct relationship to applied arts (or work that functions directly in society), are often conflated as irrelevant and are therefore belittled. Yet it is the strength of these communities, with their educational systems, international exhibitions, applied arts products, alliances and conferences that helps to breathe life into the arts. While these communities may not be viewed as current or effective by mainstream "validifiers," they support important areas of visual investigation.

The crossroads of creative insight between the artist and the mode of creation would not be connected and the artist might miss the opportunity to find her or his original voice. The Kansas City Art Institute now offers a course in zines as well as a course in etching, supporting an expanded definition of both print and design.

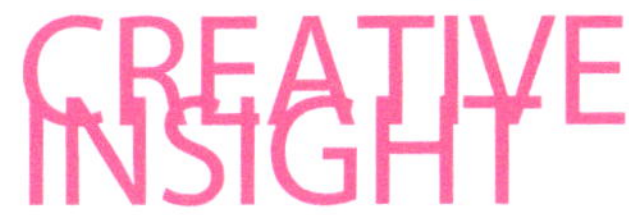

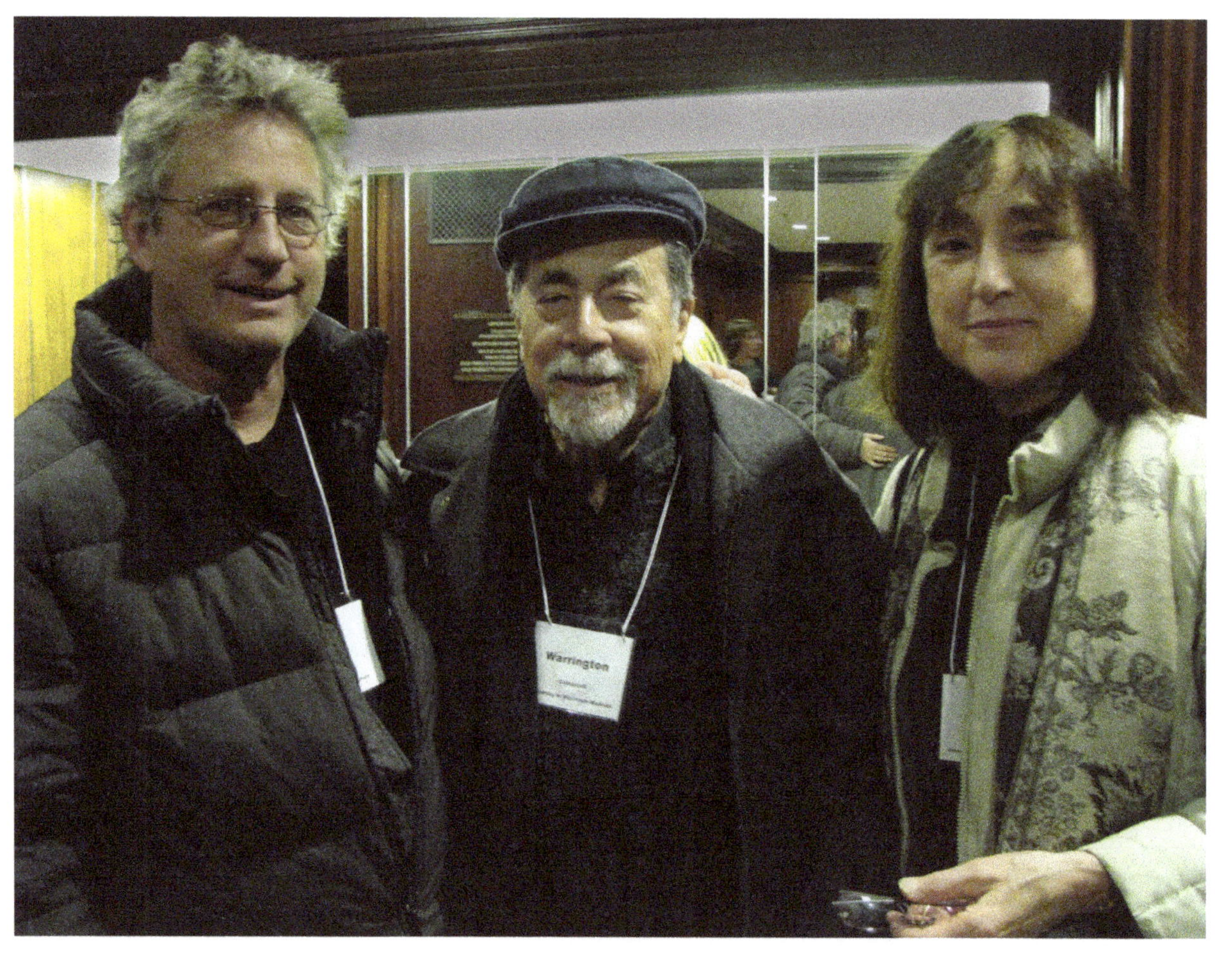

Hugh Merrill, Warrington
Colescott and Frances Myers
College Art Association
Conference
Chicago, IL
1993.

PANEL DISCUSSION

AT THE SOUTHERN GRAPHICS COUNCIL INTERNATIONAL
CONFERENCE IN CHICAGO, ILLINOIS, 1993 (3)

Much of the Quislings panel discussion focused on redefining printmaking so as to take full advantage of its cross-disciplinary nature and possibilities. The discussion divorced printmaking from the modernist aesthetics of painting, and sought to place the artist/student in a more advantageous position. The panelists believed that printmaking should be taught as a component of the expanded field of creative possibilities beyond the traditional modernist aesthetic. Opening print to a broader post-modern creative dialogue seemed to offer a solution to marginalization. The challenge of marginal status lies in expanding the territory the discipline had traditionally covered. It leads to a shift from categorizing the discipline as a set of processes: etching, relief, lithography and such. In focusing on broader issues and ideas, as several panelists noted, print was no longer marginal and printmaking issues and processes were often at the center of the most interesting contemporary work.

Barbara Kruger, Jenny Holzer and Felix Gonzales-Torres have all used printmaking strategies and processes in their creative journey, as have many other artists interested in socially engaged work. The solution presented was to claim this territory and move the educational system into a broader cross-disciplinary arena. Print could both be taught as a self-contained aesthetic territory true to its history and, simultaneously, as a road to a conceptual and post-modern practice that is not bound by the traditional hand processes or established expectations as to the shape, size and role of the print.

These issues were again raised at the 24th annual Southern Graphics Council Conference sponsored by the University of West Virginia in 2011. Frances Myers updated the Quislings panel in her presentation to the conference with co-panelist Beauvais Lyons. She pointed out that postmodern works which stem from print practices are seldom credited for their relationship to printmaking. She also pointed out that the same problems that had inspired the original panel, though somewhat reduced, still exist and the questions remain unresolved. In 2016, printmaking continues to be marginalized in its relationship to the mainstream art industry and is often misunderstood at colleges and universities.

When we speak of the marginalization of printmaking, we are speaking of the critical neglect of print by mainstream institutions, including critics, theorists, galleries, publications and museums. We are also speaking about a more general perception of artists and the arts audience. The marginalization of printmaking has broader connotations and this perception extends to other specialized disciplines that are often referred to as crafts.

In the contemporary art world, all disciplines are subject to a degree of marginalization because process and medium do not drive the development of critical theory or the next new focus. Critic David Hickey remarked to me in a discussion at the Kansas City Art Institute that "Artists will find that they (the public and the art establishment) don't care; they're just not interested. The system I describe is not corrupt; it is neither good nor bad. It is the system that has succeeded because it is deeply rooted in the evolution of American cultural and commerce. It is the system that has grown out of our culture and is not imposed on it. The team that loses the Super Bowl is marginalized and tagged a loser."

In this situation, the marginalization of disciplines is a given, and the artist working in either printmaking or painting must understand that

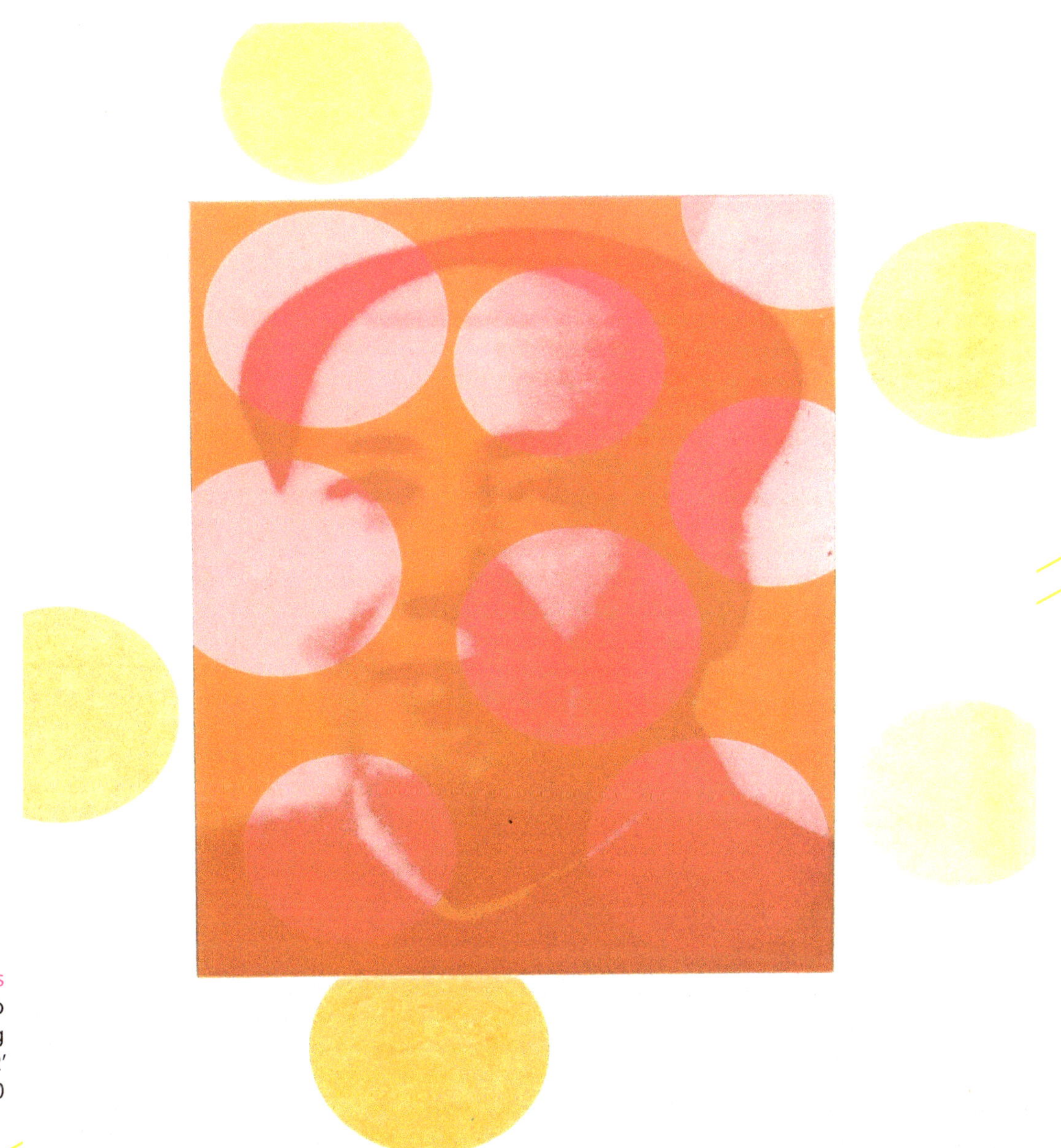

Frances Myers
Pink Mao
Etching
9' x 12'
2000

photo courtesy of Warrington Colescott

the status assigned to the discipline is not the status consigned to them as artists. The ideas and vision formulated by the artist coming out of the discipline are the criteria that will determine their acceptance and the range of their work.

In the end there are no Quislings, but there are many tricksters, magicians and outlaws. Some keep the name printmaker (Tom Huck), others evade it (Kara Walker), and some throw it away, as no past category fits (Damian Hirst). In the end Tom Huck succeeds because he can create amazing images and cut a wood block like Dürer. Kara Walker succeeds because her work is disturbingly provocative and beautiful. Hirst succeeds because of his ability to use and manipulate culture and finance. Marginalization does not mean that the community is insignificant and lacking richness; it means that the community or discipline is not of interest to the arts establishment/mainstream. Yet an artist can rise up from any discipline to be supported and collected by the elite. There is no sure road to ephemeral success or deeper cultural vision. First, you just have to make the art that lives within your own awareness and imagination.

IN THE END THERE ARE NO QUISLINGS, BUT THERE ARE MANY TRICKSTERS, MAGICIANS AND OUTLAWS.

THE MARGINALIZATION
OF PRINTMAKING

Another Look, or the 2/3 View.

Printmaking is a contradiction for being both marginalized and universally accepted. To understand this phenomenon, the discipline needs to be divided into three areas. Printmaking has entered the mainstream of contemporary art as both the creative method of the lone printmaker and the collaborative creative dialogue between master printer and artist. Mass media printing and the dissemination of everything from newspapers to commercial packaging form an ocean of images in which we swim.

1 Printmaking is all the printed images by which we communicate who we are, what's for sale and where we are going. Endless multiples of magazines and newspapers displayed on kiosks in Paris in the early 1900s were a source of inspiration spurring the cubists' investigation of pictorial space. Printmaking's mass productive process allows the artist to move away from the creation of unique and individual objects to the creation of images that communicate in the realm of popular culture to a worldwide audience.

Much of the most dynamic work of the past thirty years has been generated from mass printing as a source and process. The works being created using these sources are seldom referred to as printmaking, yet they conceptually and technically fall under the umbrella of the discipline. Pop art, Fluxus and much of Dada are printmaking phenomena as both sources and methods of articulation. Sheppard Fairy's Obey Giant and Don Ed Hardy's flash-styled tattoo graphics function as high art, covering both buildings and t-shirts.

Mass media print is also a resource, so representing the alteration of cultural branding by artists is fundamental in both modernist and postmodern creative investigations. Romare Bearden's collages made from newspapers and magazines, capturing the experience of life and music in Harlem, New York, or many of Robert Rauschenberg's prints, rubbings, silkscreens and transfers that borrow from commercial sources illustrate a link between fine art and popular culture.

Printmaking's industrial and collaborative means of production has provided a model for replacing the individual artist's hand, gesture and creation of a unique object. Barbara Kruger's Your Body is a Battle-ground (1989) was printed and placed as a provocative broadside along construction site fences in New York City to reach the eyes of the public, not the eyes of the art establishment.

Kruger's re-contextualization of commercial products and traditional portraiture encourages society to question a perceived value system. Kruger's work not only calls attention to what she sees as inherent sexism, but also emphasizes the glibness with which we consume it. The slick, motorized images seduce us into a landscape of contrast and violence where we feel at home, yet uncomfortable.

Print's second well-accepted mainstream component is the publication of blue chip artists by collaborative print studios. The history of the contemporary print is enriched and expanded by the research performed through this partnership.

It is here that print was reinvented to meet the needs of contemporary artists originally working in a variety of non-print processes. Here, common ground is discovered between print's collaborative nature and the individual vision of the artist. Methods of production were invented that took print out of traditional aesthetic confines, creating vibrant and expansive works of art.

Richard Field, noted author and print curator of the Yale Museum of Art, felt strongly that the collaborative print was the only meaningful form for the media. Like the commercial print industry, the published print is driven by market concerns. The large publication studio can only exist due to the high retail value of the collaborative print. The publication shop could not exist as it does without a large capital investment and profitable returns on the products it produces. These outcomes are an outgrowth of the economic vitality of the art market over the past fifty years.

Prints that were conceived of as being within the means of many folks have reached prices starting in the tens of thousands of dollars. Prints were generally small and intimate in the first half of the 1900s, but with Rauschenberg's Booster (1967), followed by other large-scale pieces, prints have taken on architectural spaces once reserved for paintings and sculptures. These works successfully compete for wall space in museums worldwide, hanging prominently in main galleries, not in the museum's print gallery or study room.

3   Printmaking is part of an international community that includes universities, independent print artists and regional print societies. Worldwide, there are print publications, blogs, websites and other social media networks that tie printmakers together. A vast community of artists, curators, writers, museum directors, arts administrators and volunteers facilitate events such as the Krakow Print Triennial, Krakow, Poland; Guanlan Print Biennial, Shenzhen, China; and the Impact International Printmaking Conference.

This international community is linked to universities worldwide, where print flourishes as a creative and intellectual discipline. Art departments base their educational structure on the liberal arts ideal. The visual arts disciplines are divided into departments: printmaking, ceramics, fiber, sculpture, etc. Each department produces a historic, creative and conceptual structure to investigate the discipline and the broader contemporary world.

The university is the sanctuary of the artist printmaker, and it is here that printmaking thrives as an aesthetic, craft, historical and contemporary creative possibility. The Southern Graphics Council International, the largest print group internationally, has grown out of this system.

These printmaking programs mentor students who move into all areas of the broader print community as artists, master printers, curators, writers, administrators, community art facilitators and more. Young people reinvent the discipline and its focus, taking it to unexpected places. In the past decade, young printmakers have forged new connections

between artist and audience. Cannonball Press and the Outlaw Printmakers create community events, parades and even bonfires connecting relief printing with community celebrations. Adriane Herman and Brian Reeves' Slop Art project uses commercially printed grocery-style circulars to connect art and artists to everyday life, bringing art down to a saleable product without the pretense of higher, elite values. Print has been at the forefront of the development of socially engaged art and relational aesthetics.

Though we speak of printmaking as being marginalized, the international community of arts professionals, independent artists, universities and regional print societies existing outside the concerns of the art establishment constitutes a strong support mechanism. This is the choir to which we preach, and what a beautiful and energetic choir it is. This part of the discipline will always have to contend with its outside status, living in the margins.

In spite of the status imposed by the art establishment, printmaking and the university system in general facilitate a vibrant cultural contribution. It is important to recognize the reality of this situation and build on the strengths of dwelling outside the system. Often, what is written in the margins of a document and left out of the official edited text is by far the best and most truthful content. The one who disrupts the norm always lives in the margins.

June 1996, revised in March 2016

THE ONE WHO DISRUPTS
THE NORM ALWAYS
LIVES IN THE MARGINS.

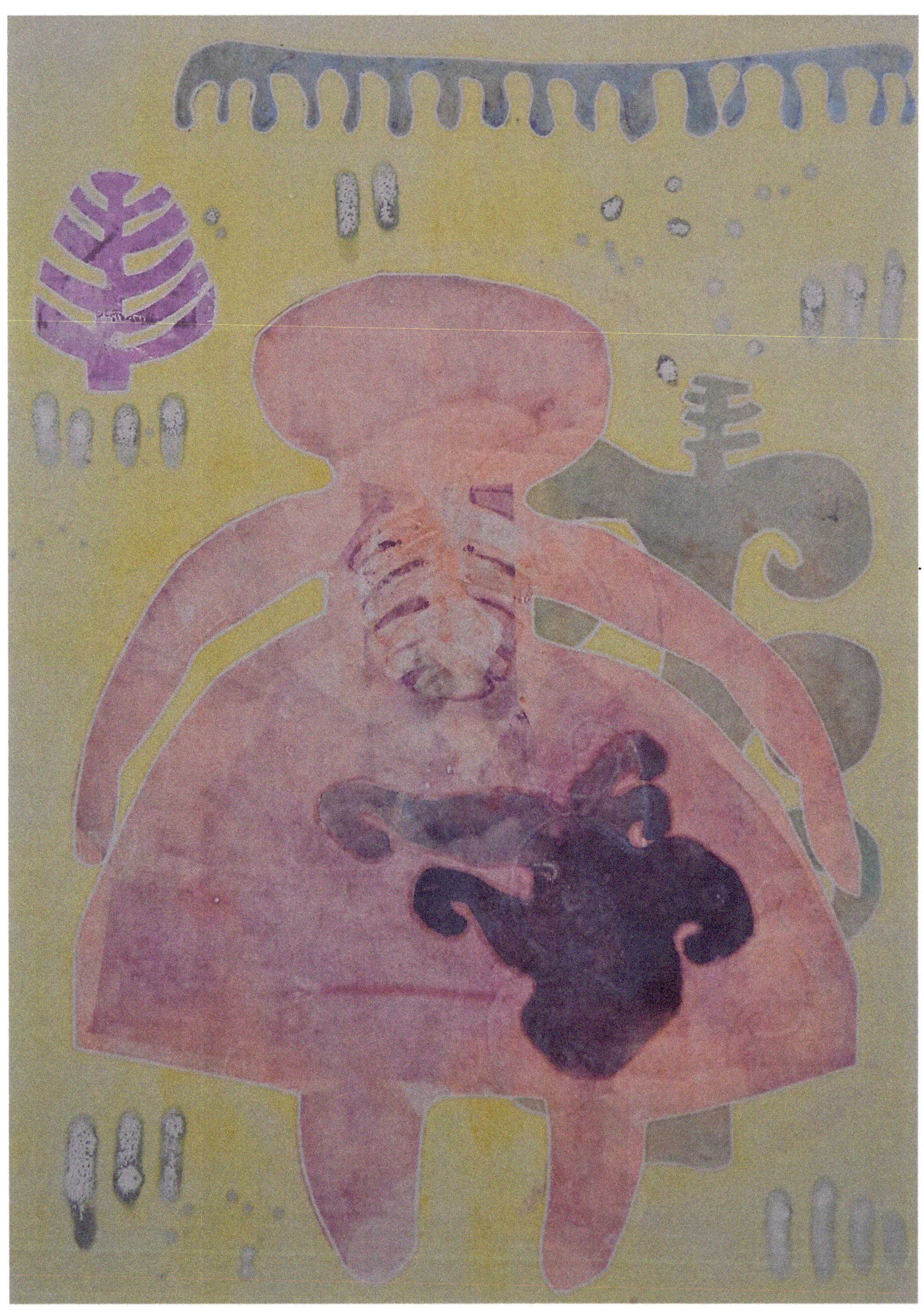

Melanie Yazzie of the Salt Water Clan and Bitter Water Clan of the Diné people of North Eastern Arizona.

Yazzie often takes part in collaborative projects with indigenous artists both nationally and internationally.

Her work is included in these and other collections: The Museum of History and Art, Anchorage, Alaska; The Missoula Art Museum in Missoula, Montana; and the Kennedy Museum of Art at Ohio University in Athens, Ohio.

Of her journeys, she says, "It's at these gatherings and traveling from place to place that fuels my work and revitalizes my spirit."

I try in my own way to help people connect by organizing print exchanges on a variety of themes. My own art work strives to educate people on many levels about issues related to my life as a Native American woman. I have worked hard to become a professor of printmaking and I am proud to teach people about printmaking at the University of Colorado at Boulder!

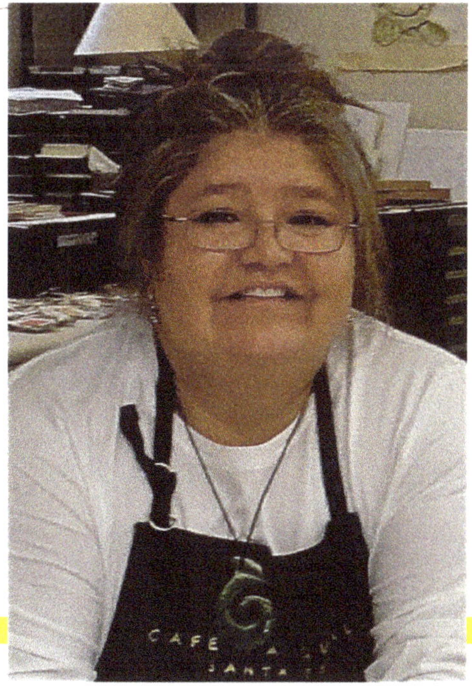

Melanie Yazzie
Pollen Girl
Monotype
42" x 30"
2013

photo courtesy of the artist

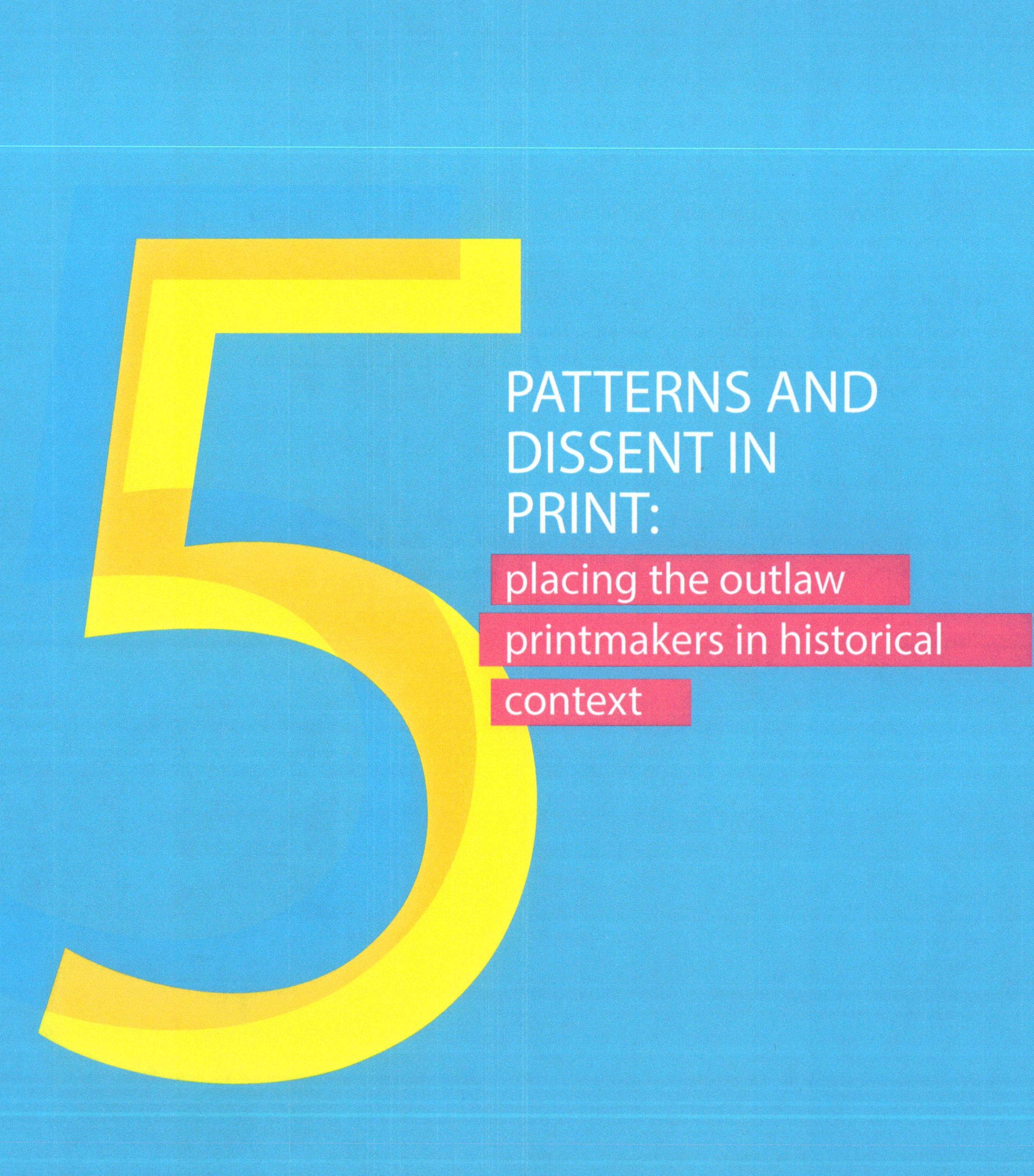

5

PATTERNS AND DISSENT IN PRINT:

placing the outlaw printmakers in historical context

WHAT CONSTITUTES AN OUTLAW?

By definition, an outlaw is someone who operates outside the law. Yet, in America, the outlaw is more than a criminal, murderer, or thief. Outlaws are often portrayed in romantic songs and stories as robbing from the rich and giving to the poor. In popular culture, they rise above today's economic and political terrorists to be more than Bernie Madoff, Pablo Escobar, or Osama Bin Laden.

A mix of history, reality, and mythology, outlaws use violent or illegal means to gain an advantage for themselves at the expense of others. Who are these others? They are not the investors scammed by Bernie Madoff's scheme which destroyed the lives of individuals. More often, outlaws attack authority: the cops, the banks, the unfair, tilted system. Outlaws are more heroes than burglars, highwaymen or thieves. Online and popular culture portray Jesse James, Robin Hood, Blackbeard, Bonnie and Clyde as fitting this mold. In movies, we see outlaws in Easy Rider, The Dead Poet's Society and On the Waterfront.

Country musicians are perhaps the best example of outlaw artists who realize their individual expression, reinvigorate history, and connect to an older notion of purity while pushing the edges of opinion and directly taking on the established system. Highly successful singers, such as Waylon Jennings, Merle Haggard, Willie Nelson, David Allan Coe, Townes Van Zandt, and Steve Earle, are among the outlaws of country music— artists who easily cross the line between being country stars and cultural pains in the ass while pushing the music in their own visionary directions.

Art has no laws, but it does have a series of limitations, restrictions, and expectations placed on it by society, museums, critics, theorists, the academic world and commercial concerns. These restrictions are especially important in university and art college programs where students hope to progress in their artistic development.

Within the snake-pit of academic thinking, painting has died numerous deaths since the 1960s. Ceramics, printmaking, and other disciplines are often found to be irrelevant crafts, as is working with materials and techniques in general. Still, art schools continue to be filled with young printmakers, ceramicists and painters. For decades, concepts, theory, words, explanations, and discussions have eclipsed the activity of making art or objects in importance, but artists continue to make things.

Every year, universities and colleges fill with young artists, many paying a small fortune, who want to learn to draw, paint, mold ceramic forms and make prints. They are often confronted by academic assertions that imagery is dead, figure drawing is passé, craft and skill have little value, the copy is more important than the original, the hand-made mark is out and so on. It is not that postmodern or conceptual concerns do not have value, but many times, they do not express the breadth and depth of artistic and creative practice. The high value placed on thinking and concepts casts aside a huge field of creative activity as devalued.

As young artists move through the academic system, many fail to self-identify with a perceived or actual over-intellectualization, which they see as an establishment cover-up. They sometimes seek a means of making tied more closely to realization than strategies. They often delve into the absurd, dreams, surrealism, or non-linear constructions of images and thoughts. These young artists might look for ways of making that defy explanation, seeking a balance between chance and organization, between body and mind. The sources from which they work and the way their art enters society are also called into question. Often, these artists shy away from the critical gallery venue where art is sold to the 1% and, instead, look for venues closer to the community, on the street, or through friends. With ease, they move up and down the scale from fine art to commercial products, making both prints sold to collectors and T-shirts sold online or in pop-up shops at community events.

It is in this context that Tony Fitzpatrick and Sean Starwars founded the Outlaw Printmakers artists' group in 2000, at nearly the same time as that year's Southern Graphics Council International Conference. It is no coincidence that Tony Fitzpatrick is friends with and designs CD covers for Steve Earle, the country-music outlaw.

In 2003, Tom Huck, a former university instructor, organized a traveling exhibition of Outlaw Printmakers, including Michael Krueger, Peregrine Honig, Bill Fick, Michael Barnes, Jenny Schmid and others. The exhibitions and performance activities of the Outlaw Printmakers have led to a critical discussion of the role of the artist, the artist as entrepreneur, and the reinvigoration of basic, pure forms of relief and intaglio print process as public events. This national discussion in conferences, colleges and universities has not always been civil or kind.

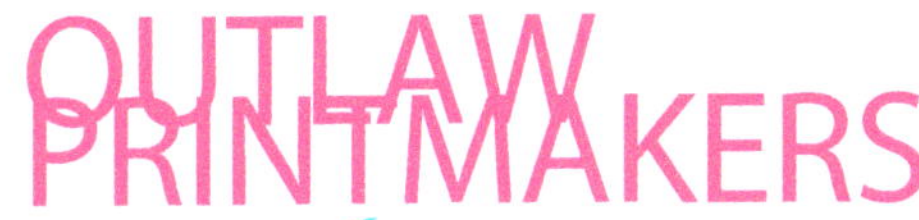

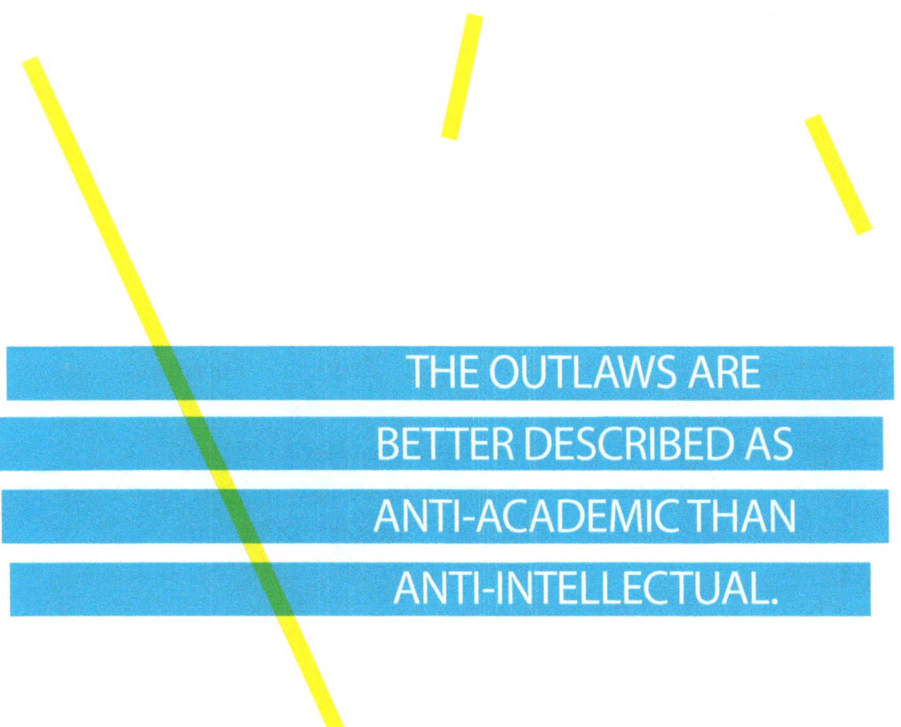
THE OUTLAWS ARE
BETTER DESCRIBED AS
ANTI-ACADEMIC THAN
ANTI-INTELLECTUAL.

OUTLAW PRINTMAKERS: ANTI-ACADEMIC TRICKSTERS

The Outlaws are better described as anti-academic than anti-intellectual. Their work and interests span a broad range of ideas, histories, and social and intellectual concerns. Many are professors and teachers at universities and colleges or are called on as substitutes for teachers on leave or sabbatical. They are regularly invited to serve as visiting artists in university art programs and are involved in conferences and other discussion forums for contemporary printmaking. These Outlaws see art education itself as a problem, so they point to their own discipline as part of a system in need of significant change. The desired change is complex but, for now, can be summed up in two concerns.

- The Outlaws see education as overly intellectual. The required acts of writing, critique, critical evaluation, and discussion are based in language and rational, linear thinking. The skills learned are to explain, decipher and articulate ideas. These skills are very different than the processes used by the Hairy Who, the Chicago Imagist, and various schools of surrealism focused on vision, experience and image. Academic intellectual approaches are believed to have become a detriment to, rather than an enrichment of, artmaking. Academic activities rooted in logical thought, not the imagination, are right-brained and interfere with the training of the mind to be visual, playful and non-linear. Often, this training leads young artists to constantly second-guess their practice, images, and ideas and, at times, to stop making art all together.

- The practicality of art education is a second point of concern. Students spend tens of thousands of dollars and end up with significant debt to attain BFA and MFA degrees that have little commercial application in broader society or the work-a-day world.

These opinions have merit as the vast majority of students who graduate with a fine arts degree do not work as artists. Approximately 10% work as artists, and another 6% in other creative fields. (1.)The career statistics for art students can be considered grim. Students in traditional genres of fine arts can be regarded as especially vulnerable. At the Kansas City Art Institute in 2002, a drawing instructor told a night class that waitressing was what the world had to offer the soon-to-be (female) graduates.

This statement alone brings into sharp focus the need for commitment, professionalism, and new programming on the part of universities, art programs and colleges to produce graduates who can take advantage of the economic system into which they are thrown. The economic and emotional costs are too high to simply dump graduates into the market, with a pat on the back while saying, "Follow your dream." If any group should be interested in whether art students can find/create work, it should be the people who supposedly help prepare them to do just that. Being a good artist/student isn't enough; artists have to be able to change the society they enter through entrepreneurial and social practice, as well as through promoting and marketing their work.

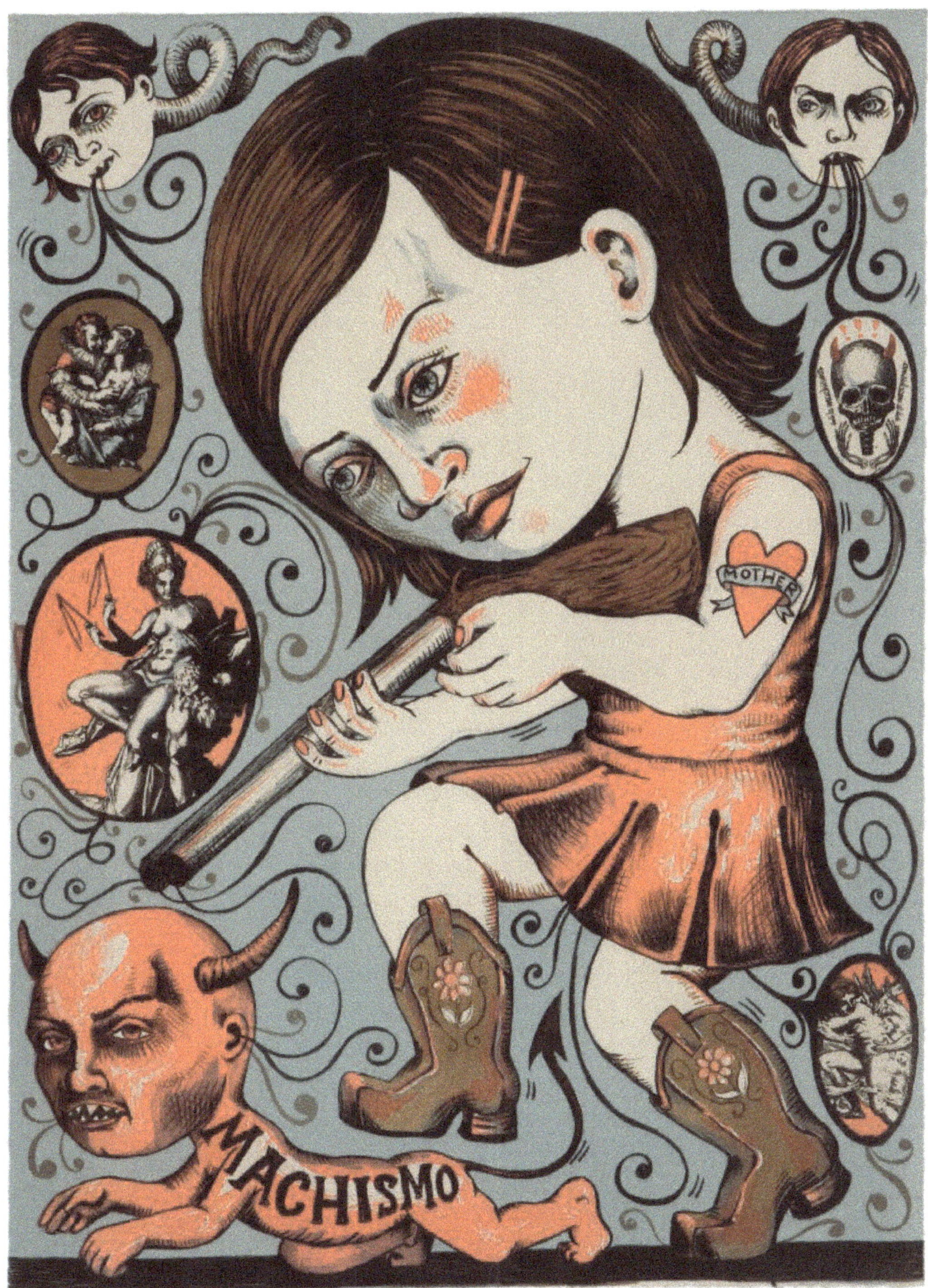

Jenny Schmid
The Pathetic Death of
Machismo
Lithograph
20" x 15"
2005

The Outlaw Printmakers deploy a number of strategies to position themselves as artists free of the narrow constraints imposed by the broader academic and mainstream arts cultures.

> The Outlaws of Printmaking, also known as The Outlaws and Outlaw Printmakers are a collective of printmaking artists that exist internationally. They formed at a show in New York in Big Cat Gallery in 2000. While searching for a name to designate this loose collective, Tony Fitzpatrick, the owner of the Big Cat Press which is associated with the gallery, decided to call it "Outlaw Printmaking" to reflect attitudes of the printmakers involved and their non-academic approach to prints. Sean Starwars elaborated that the circumstance of it is what really made it happen, since the Southern Graphics Council Conference was happening at the same time. Many of the artists associated with the movement cite the printmaker/artist Richard Mock as a primary influence. Mock's political and social narrative prints appeared in the New York Times op-ed pages for more than a decade in the 1980s and early 1990s. (2)

There are a number of points important to any discussion of printmaking Outlaws:

1   The Outlaws effectively move in and out of their own culture, combining opportunity with wit to create openings for themselves and others. They bypass, attack, and make fun of those who adhere to and administer cultural and educational structures that, in reality, often support the Outlaws' own efforts and events. The Outlaw Printmakers' satirical attack on the aesthetic confines of printmaking follows a long tradition in art and, specifically, print media. By questioning their place and function within the broader conversation on contemporary

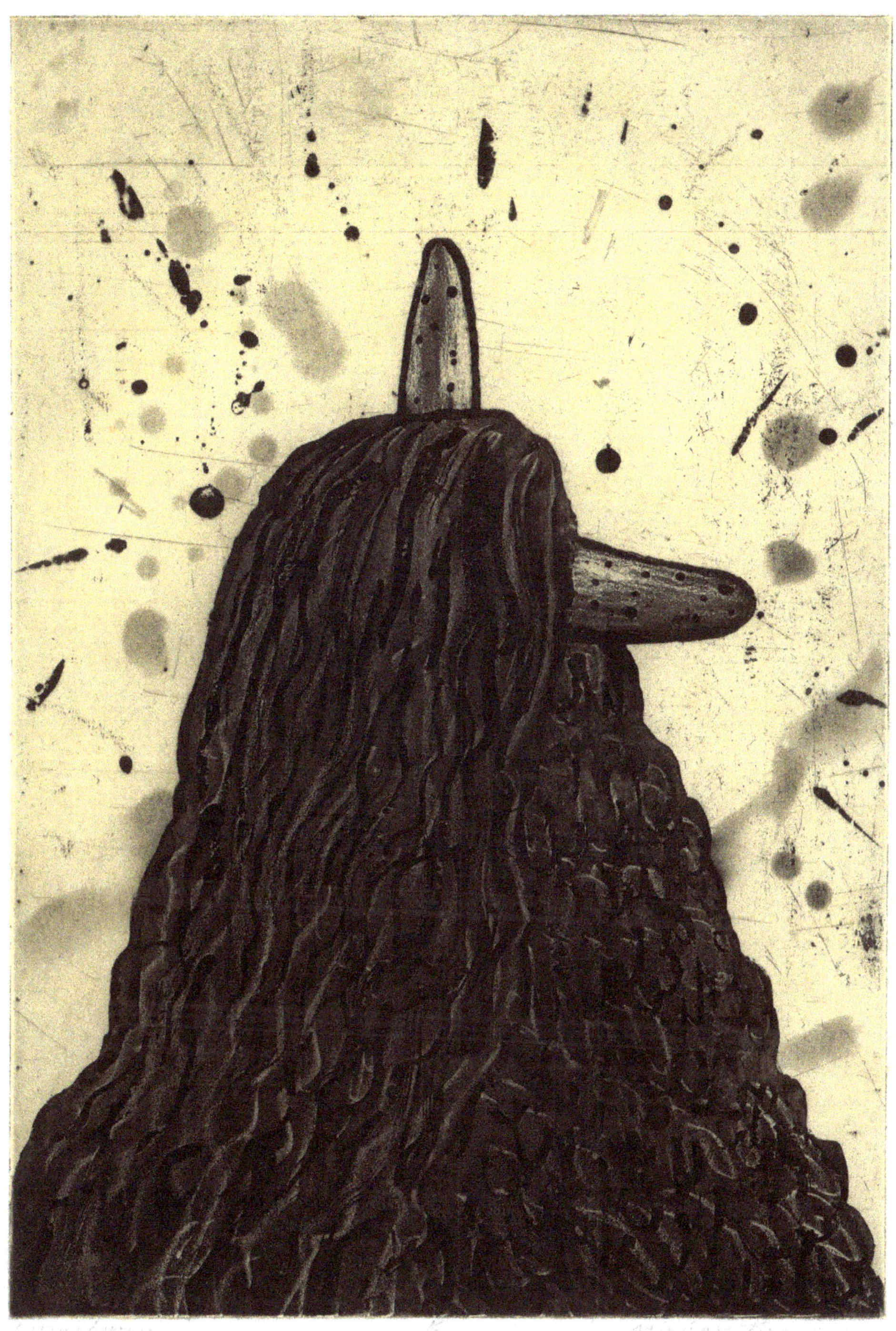

Michael Krueger
Lump Lump
intaglio Hahnemühle Dürer Etch on with
Gampi chine-collé
Image size – 13" x 9"
paper size 18" x 14"
2015
ed. 5

art, the Outlaws highlight both spontaneity and personal creativity. They also encourage a larger conversation on the true benefits and goals of academic study.

Whereas many contemporary art pieces are intended for the elite and the aesthetically knowledgeable crowd, many Outlaws go low-brow and produce T-shirts and coffee mugs for people on the street. Outlaws move effortlessly between the uplands inhabited by collectors and museum curators and the lowlands filled with tourists buying cool stuff.

2   Art is part of a public happening involving a diverse, non-arts public. The movement of artists out of the gallery museum into communities is a well-documented area of artistic and creative action. Community art, social practice and relational aesthetics are all based on the artist facilitating community and cultural interactions. They provide ritual and creative possibilities for the everyday person and reduce the distance between art and life.

Even as this community-based process has become universally accepted and taught in every major art program across the country, it remains edgy and works to attack the status quo and long-held beliefs in the individual artist/genius producing a masterpiece. Printing relief blocks in public and other events, such as parades and bonfires, challenge artists and artworks looking to become high-priced commodities for stockbrokers and investors.

3   Outlaw Printmakers assault the fundamental core beliefs of the

university system educating the next generation of artists. They see graduate and undergraduate programs as overly intellectual and wasting creative energy on critical theory, criticism and historical progression. Outlaws feel that these programs spend too much time explaining art instead of making art. Writing papers, artist statements and exercises exploring critical theory are viewed as a waste of time and effort. Outlaws see academic art as an imposter trying to be something it can't be, in direct contrast to what they envision as a more authentic mode of working.

Many Outlaws can be described as tricksters, double-crossing their way from dissing academics to accepting paychecks and awards supported by universities or affiliated organizations. A defining characteristic of the Outlaws is their distrust of the printmaking university system with its emphasis on criticism, discussion of contemporary art theory and regime of intellectual academic assignments. The Outlaws assume the guise of the imposter to attack the fundamental foundations of university scholarship, replacing them with an open-ended, subconscious approach to making and evaluating art. This perspective has a long and significant history.

This anti-talking/thinking–about–art attitude is enriched and supported by the history of expressionism and the preference for body knowledge over mental cognition. The Outlaws' work is often visionary and rarely a series of planned or designed concepts. Satirist Richard Mock cut directly on linoleum blocks with little preliminary drawing. The image is made in the act of cutting, constructing a direct connection between the artist's hand, the material and the subconscious image coming into existence.

This viewpoint is also supported by the purity of the outside artist without formal cultural training who makes amazing works free of the theoretical debates in contemporary art. For the Outlaw, art comes as a vision from the subconscious, chance and stimulation rather than conscious, analytical thought.

4   Imagery is connected to the history of print as a medium of satire and political attack, similar to Daumier and Sue Coe. Not only is their methodology the same as the trickster, but their message often attacks whatever they see as the status quo and traditional power structures.

5   This approach represents a direct and purposeful attack on the structures that serve to nurture and support the Outlaws. They do what all good tricksters do, not letting the culture in which they grew up escape disruption and reinvention while working to loosen the bonds that solidify thought and practice.

ART COMES AS A VISION FROM THE SUBCONSCIOUS

Entrepreneurship is nearly essential to anyone making and marketing work today. Even if an artist secures good gallery representation, there is endless work to procure venues and work out the logistics of proposed and actual exhibitions. In most traditional art school environments, only the problems of art itself are addressed. Much time is devoted to theory and ideas. The idea of finding a way to continue your work after leaving art school is touched upon by some instructors but abhorred by others who believe that a class in professional practice training consists of demonstrating how to stretch a canvas or perhaps learning how to build a shipping crate.

The disconnection between art school and the "real world" leaves graduates with only part of the skills they need to hone to market and promote their work. The art itself is the easy part. The money and employment part of the equation is much more difficult. Very few artists get what they should for their work, considering the time, effort and cost of materials to produce it. Many young artists possess few social and communication skills, which are essential when interfacing with potential clients.

The art itself
is the easy part.

The Outlaws have navigated the making of art and the making of money to support the art habit as well as any group while also developing a significant community and cultural impact. The Outlaws and their extended family—Cannonball Press, Swoon, Drive by Press and others—continue to find new outlets and connections for their vision. From Dennis McNett's skateboard decks and John Hitchcock's street signs to museum exhibitions and sales to collectors, printmakers continually demonstrate the interlocking potential of both art and commerce.

The ingenuity and success of the Outlaws and the distance they have created between their lives and work and academic art education beg many large questions that have yet to be answered or even discussed. For example, if 84% of art school graduates do not end up in careers in the arts, where do they go? Was the education they received of value in getting there? In short, is the BFA of more benefit to the student who does not become an artist? If so, then how should art education change to reflect this reality? This text is not intended to explore this issue, but it is a culturally and economically relevant question called to attention by the entrepreneurial success and cultural impact of the Outlaws and studios, such as Tom Huck's Evil Prints, Sean Starwars' Woodcut Funhouse and Jenny Schmid's Bikini Press International.

Printmaking, like all other locally understood webs of significance, has accepted paradigmatic patterns which have changed significantly over time. In 1968, many graduate schools viewed as suspect the authenticity of color etchings and lithographs as genuine art, while monotypes and monoprints were regarded as marginal as well. Copier prints were non-existent in the print community. Silkscreen was still considered a commercial process. Over the next ten years, these aesthetic assumptions would be turned upside down by printmaker tricksters broadening the range of the discipline. The Outlaws are merely a passing but important energy in the print history and community, helping to extend, reinvent and refocus the discipline. They are preceded and supported by a history of artists embedded in a socially and politically active mindset. From Daumier to Hogarth, Beckman to Huck, printmaking has a long history of rustling the feathers of politicians and the public alike. In this way, the Outlaw Printmakers have deep historical precedents, and their work continues unabated, engaging new generations of artists and art students.

THE ART ITSELF IS THE EASY PART. THE MONEY AND EMPLOYMENT PART OF THE EQUATION IS MUCH MORE DIFFICULT.

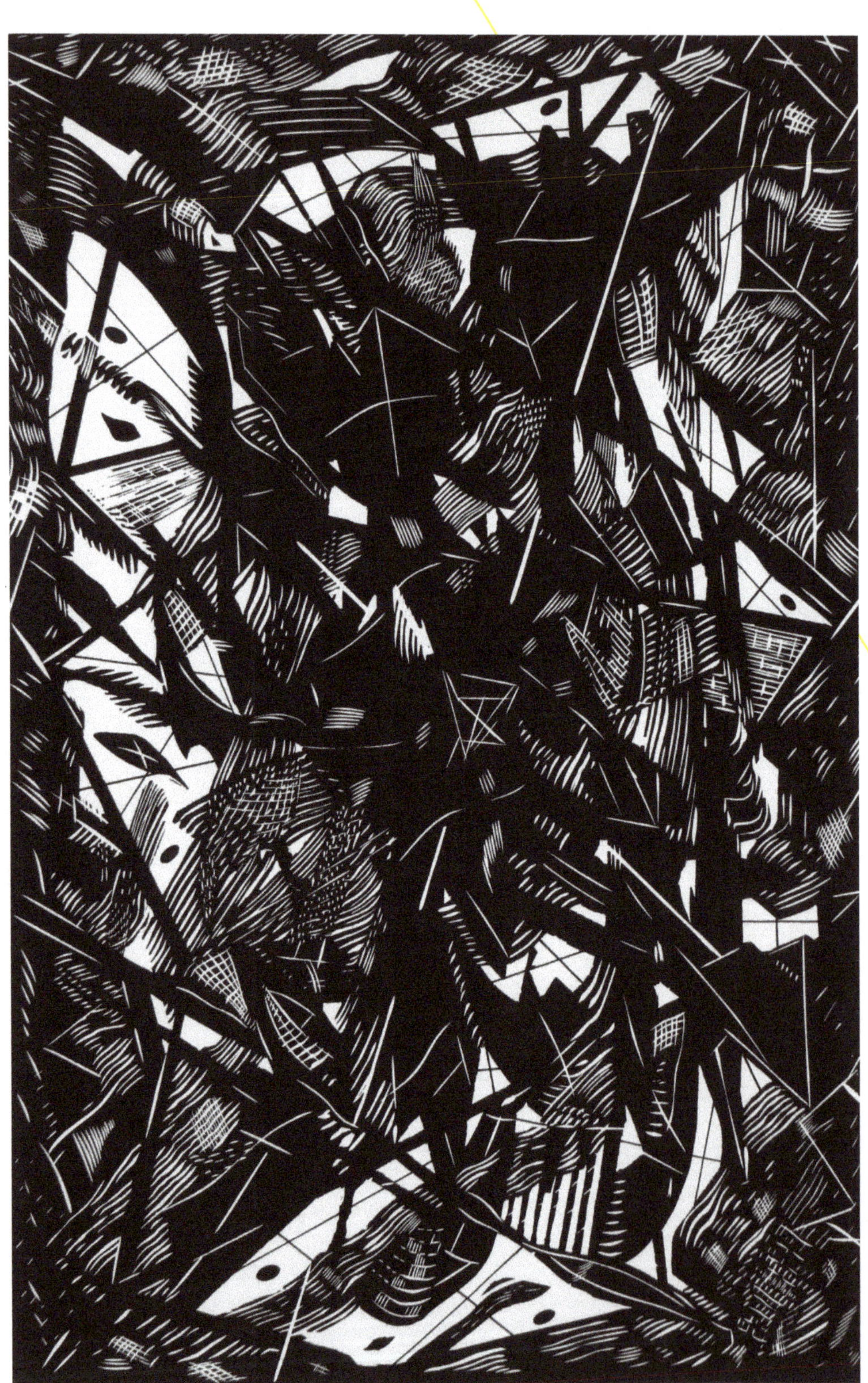

Hugh Merrill
China Twist
woodcut/engraving
on Kozo paper
24" x 42"
2014

Over the course of two residencies at the Guanlan Printmaking
Base in Shenzhen, China, in 2012 and 2014, Merrill worked on a series
of wood relief engravings. In the late 1980s, he produced several
series of large relief prints and monotypes. It was an investigation
that seemed unresolved, and he felt a new approach was needed.
Like much of Merrill's work, it is related to spatial complexity and
landscape. The following prints were printed in editions of 15 and
are in the Guanlan Museum of Printmaking.

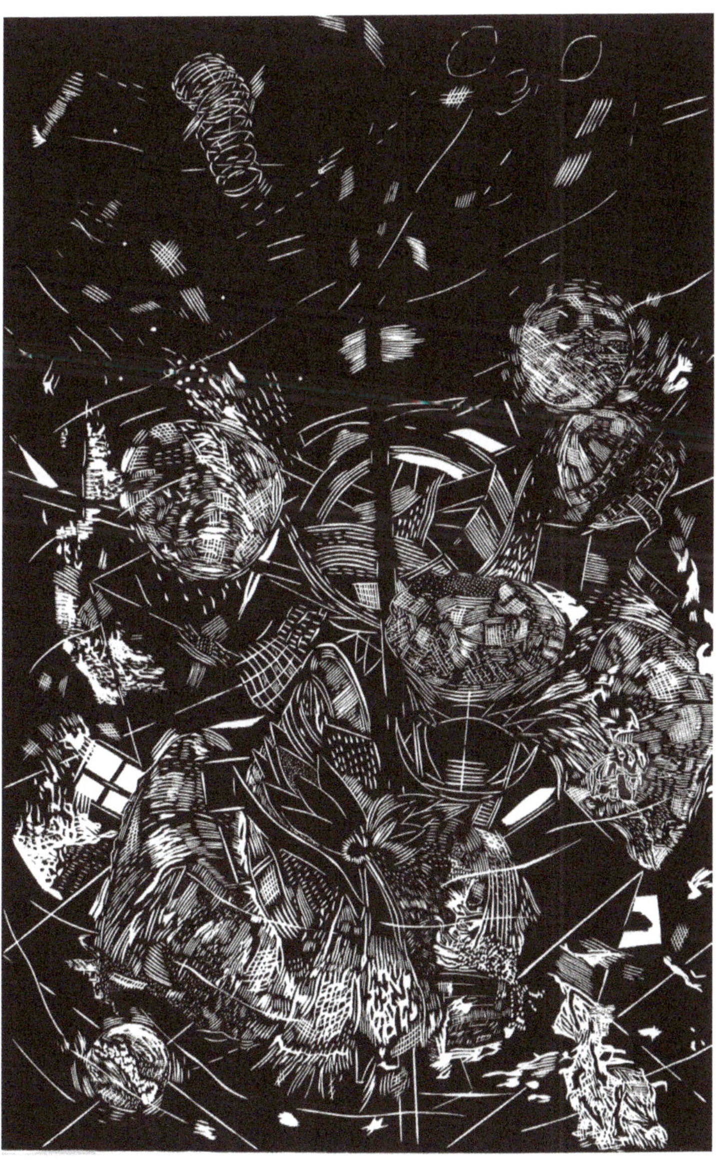

Hugh Merrill
Kiki's World
woodcut/engraving
on Kozo paper
24" x 42"
2014

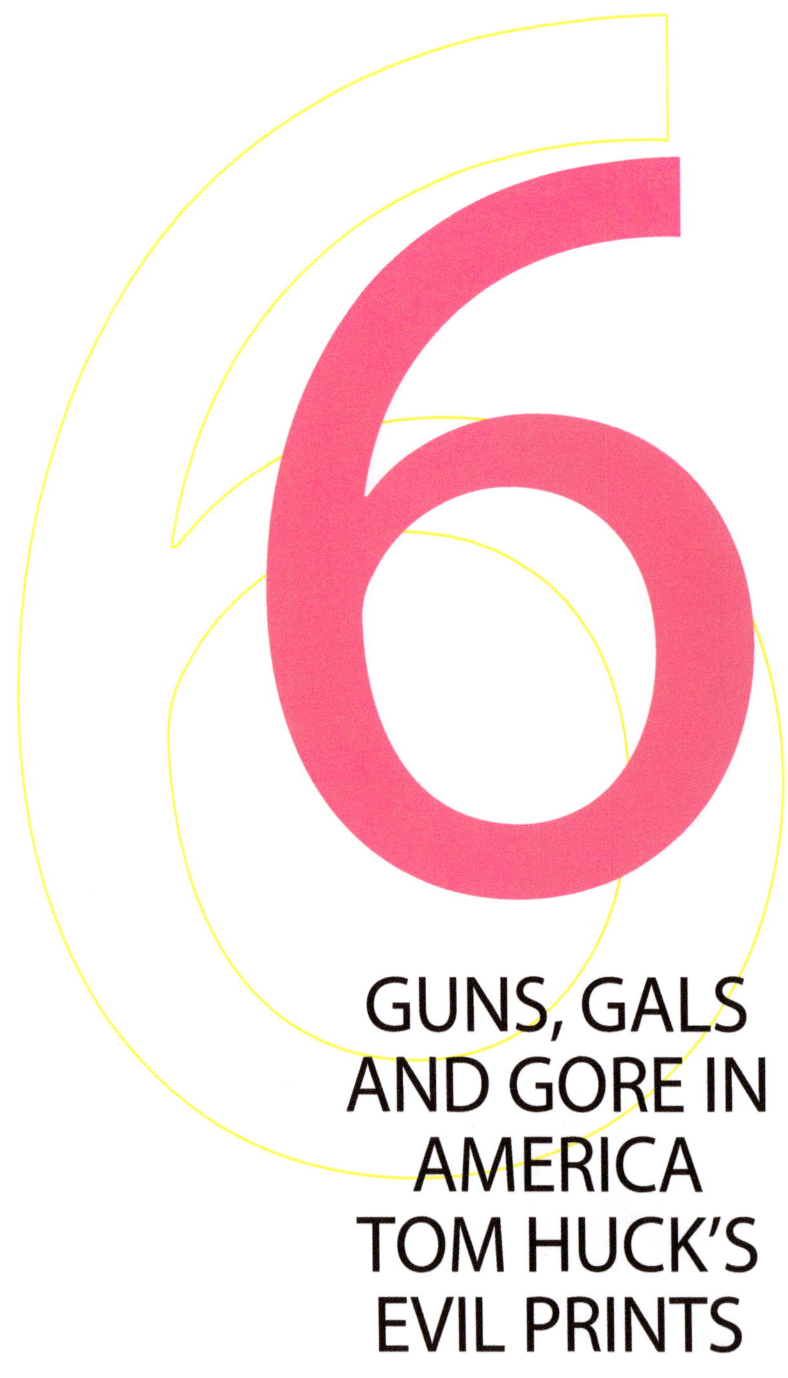

6

GUNS, GALS AND GORE IN AMERICA TOM HUCK'S EVIL PRINTS

WHEN ARTISTS, CRITICS, theorists and institutions solidify artistic investigation into a closed and self-assured set of rules, other ideas will rise up. There are lines of creative thought that run deep within the human experience. One of these is the need to attack and disrupt the status quo, the certainty of art history's canon-makers and the condescension of those in the know.

From the artistic screams spurred by the bloody disaster of World War I, to the Hairy Who, a group in the 1960s that demanded freedom from the strictures of the New York School of painting. The need for alternatives to traditional voices has always been present. Today, within the Outlaws Printmakers there is a deep-seated need for artists to be rebellious, independent thinkers. The late critic, Hilton Kramer, writing about the Chicago Imagist in the New York Times, bemoaned "a woeful scarcity of serious aesthetic inquiry" in the work of the Hairy Who. (1) This group of artists did not give a damn for Hilton Kramer's permission, enthusiasm or opinion as they continued their investigations.

Unlike former art movements that are often held together by formulistic concerns for style such as cubism, abstract expressionism or minimalism, those that strike out on their own are defined by individualism, as tricksters and clowns reordering the content and mark suitable for high art. They jab and box, fighting to create space and time to make their work in the capitalist commercial system of artistic production. Often they succeed in spite of the difficulty of fitting into the present paradigm in which they exist and work.

Adelia Ganson, in her interview with Tom Huck, has captured the spirit of the outsider, imagists and others from which Tom Huck and so many other independent artists have been nurtured.

—Hugh Merrill, February 2016.

ALL HUCKED UP: GUNS, GALS AND GORE IN AMERICA

The art of Tom Huck is sure to offend many. This art is not for the politically correct, the faint of heart, or the easily offended. Huck has been disgusting the masses since 1995, so he's had a long time to build up his impact on the public. If you don't find something here a little to your dislike, or at least to make you breathe in fast and laugh a bit, the artist has not succeeded. Even the most open-minded person is sure to find a bit of distaste here.

How does an artist reach a point where they don't care who dislikes, is offended by, or just jumps back from a particular image? Huck relishes and craves this reaction. The answer; an extremely self-confident and well developed sense of self and internal vision, coupled with a distinct knowledge of one's place in art history, A high level of technical expertise makes all of this possible.

This is not the type of work that invites everyone in. It observes society, filters and interprets it. Like many aspects of "real-life" it's not pretty. It's gruesome, detailed, dark, and takes place in the night. These characters are bound by shadow and characterization not possible in the light of day. To add to the dramatic effect, the pieces are printed with black ink on white paper.

The black and white palette happens for a reason, well planned and executed with a technical precision worthy of this modern master. This work can be compared to the "old masters" of woodcut and be competitive, if not superior. His technical precision is quite astonishing, as is easily seen in the printing plates. Interestingly, his images are made with one piece of wood, as opposed to several different plates printed at different times to produce an image.

Where Tom Huck lives, real revenge is possible. Remember that time at your cousin's bachelor party where the stripper walked out on stage and reminded you of an awkward pregnant, unattractive girl with cellulite? And you had actually had to pay a cover charge to get in to see her? Maybe you should have driven a little farther, to a different city or a more expensive club? Or the time the guy on the kid's bicycle cut you off and nearly caused an insurance claim? You remember, the guy with the thing on his head, a ski mask or something else.

They are all skewered, slathered with sauce and grilled to perfection in Huck's work, a scathing and detailed account of Americans, in all their idiosyncratic, awkward and grisly glory.

It makes me feel better just looking at them, giggling, and remembering. They are the same people I see at the Wal-Mart, or at my local Hot Pots café. I see them driving trucks and less frequently, cars with strong opinions in stickers attached to the back window. "You'll take my gun over my cold dead body" or something similar.

THEY ARE ALL SKEWERED, SLATHERED WITH SAUCE AND GRILLED TO PERFECTION...

Looking at these pieces serves as a form of release. In the artist's Bloody Bucket series (2002) his iconic work Possum Promenade is sure to cause the viewer to wince as they realize they may have caught a glimpse of someone at a reception or county fair with the same enthusiasm for a similar event. Maybe they were on their way back from the cleaning section at Walmart when they stopped by.

There is a strong element of recognition within this piece that's very easily seen. In this series, produced in 2002 "hillbillies" are doing very bad things, and they are depicted with a sense of glee.

Bed of Bones, based on a true story of two lesbian lovers that were found with hundreds of dead dogs in their house, brings to mind a news story of a "hoarder house" in Illinois where a dead body was found. It also mirrors many stories of abused or neglected pets. These stories can be seen daily on cable television, and appear frequently in newspapers.

One of the interesting things about Huck's work is that many of the pieces are indeed based on specific realities, they are not made up. Huck is a native Missourian, born and raised in Potosi, he now lives and works in St.. Louis, where his shop, Evil Prints, is located. He works with a volunteers staff of seven other people, and hosts workshops and classes for interested artists. Evilprints currently teaches relief, silkscreen, etching and mixed media in a 3,500 square foot facility.

He taught at Washington University in St. Louis for over ten years before leaving the school, which he describes as "awful" and he describes his fellow academics as "shallow, mediocre, and devoid of ambition."

MAYBE THEY WERE ON THEIR WAY BACK FROM THE CLEANING SECTION AT WALMART WHEN THEY STOPPED BY.

THE ARTIST'S WORK IS FIRMLY ROOTED IN THE CATEGORY OF POLITICAL SATIRE.

Huck's artistic lineage goes back to the 1400's, with the artist Albrecht Dürer, who was born in 1471. Like Huck, he is seen as an innovator within the media of the woodcut, and possessed a very specific style unmistakable to viewers. He is also very influenced by the artists William Hogarth as well as Yoshitoshi, Rembrandt van Rijn and George Grosz.

Hogarth was a Britist artist (b. 1697 d. 1764) credited with pioneering western sequential art, he is also acknowledged as an ancestor of the comic strip. Much like Huck, he was known to use the characters in his work for social criticism, and he also pioneered efforts to help artists become independent of wealthy patrons, by producing engravings of his paintings. Hogarth's work is often compared to the work of dramatic writers in subject matter.

With all this history behind him, I wonder how these images relate to today's politics. According to the artist, in his early pieces, the characters were from a specific place in Missouri where the artist lived as a youth. Although he had a happy childhood, having a highly developed sense of art, and visual aesthetics, he could tell he was a person a bit out of place, not exactly like the rest of the neighborhood. He attended Southern Illinois University as an undergraduate, and Washington University in St. Louis as an MFA candidate.

The artist's work is firmly rooted in the category of political satire. The French artist Honore Daumier (b 1808, d. 1879) produced politically oriented works in France in the 1700's. He was incarcerated at one point for making them. Printmakers have long been know for their ability to express strong opinions in humorous, provocative ways.

Huck continues this tradition with his "Outlaw Printmakers" series of exhibitions. When I asked him about the project, Huck says:

> "The outlaw printmakers were named by Tony Fitzpatrick, while I was having a conversation with him about new attitudes in printmaking. This was in the early 2000s. Its not really a project, but a bunch of my buddies who do non-academic, hard core imagery that is influenced by the darker side of things, like metal, horror movies, and posters. Myself, Sean Starwars, Bill Fick, and a host of others are lumped in to this group, but that's fine with me. The whole thing was started by Richard Mock, really. He was like the Posada of the 80s and 90s, making a linocut a day and then putting them in the op-ed page of the New York Times. He was a real hard living, hard working printmaker and he influenced me and my friends greatly. The whole outlaw thing is really about making no compromises in your imagery and emphasizing the dark and lurid because that's where we feel we're at as a society. As printmakers, like our forefathers we want to be a reflection of the times we live in, like Hogarth."

The work he is producing now is more relevant on a national level, as opposed to being set in the Midwest, he sees it now in a larger context, the whole of the United States. So what does it all mean? Is all this visual revenge simply a satirical view of the general public in America, or is it something else? Do these pieces encourage dialogue about the people in this country, their prejudices, foibles and flaws? What is the best way to interpret these images of gore and violence? Perhaps they remind us that we may be connected to these characters in some way. By being present in our society, do they somehow reflect on us, perhaps as a mirror of something darker and more disturbing than we are comfortable with.

They remind us a little of people we actually know. People we don't just see in cars or at McDonald's, but something else, something closer, close enough to make us uncomfortable. Close enough to give us goosebumps and grimace a little. The way the faces on the subjects in the artworks are similar gives them the impression of the everyman, and yet, by their similarity, they represent no one specific. This double reflection helps us to understand that just underneath the surface, things can look very different.

Huck possessed a finely honed ability to look at society as a whole with the knowledge that for everything that appears clean, pretty and sanitized, there is also an opposite reality that is always present. These characters appear throughout our daily lives, we pass them on the street, and we see them at the store. We have learned that

The work he is producing now is more relevant on a national level, as opposed to being set in the Midwest, he sees it now in a larger context, the whole of the United States.

just below the surface of beauty lies a starker place that has been tapped into and brought forth into the light of day.

So why woodcut? The artist comments:

> "Woodcuts are an inherently expressive medium. By that I mean when one carves and image out of wood it fights you. God or whatever didn't make trees for us to carve images out of, and that struggle shows in the resulting printed image. This is why the German expressionists loved woodcuts so much, for it heightened the emotional content of the work. The quality of the lines are more jagged, and heavy black. Another big reason: DÜRER!"

We want to turn away, yet can't stop looking. We are entertained and perhaps shocked as we spend time with the work. When my daughter was 8 years old, she saw Beef Brain Buffet at the gallery where I worked. When she was 16, 8 years later, she confessed she had nightmares about the piece for several years. According to Huck, this is exactly the reaction he seeks.

Tom Huck
Possum Promenade
from The Bloody Bucket suite
Woodcut
52' x 38'
2001-2005

photo courtesy of the artist

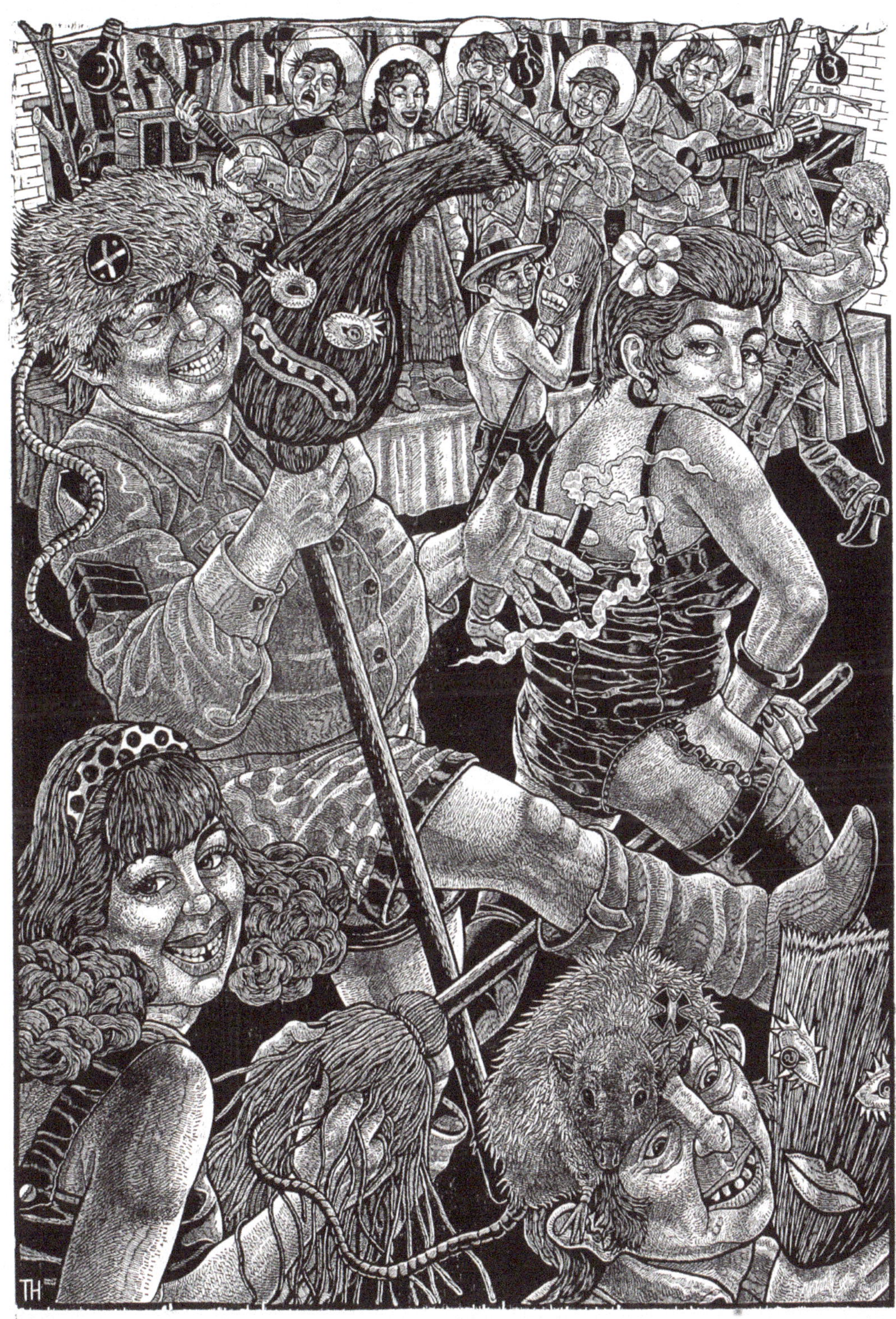

When Shelby and I started this project we envisioned a rather standard academic book. A table of contents, listing a series of essays on contemporary printmaking. Where one ended on the next page the next essay began. As we played with the design, we felt the book should be a celebration of Printmaking and the amazing print community. So the cover became hot pink, images by friends were added, and playful design elements were woven in. We decided that instead of placing this bio at the end of the book, it should become part of the text. Here is who we are. Please feel free to contact me if you have questions or discussion points regarding the book, and we hope you will greatly enjoy our effort.

—Hugh Merrill

HUGH MERRILL

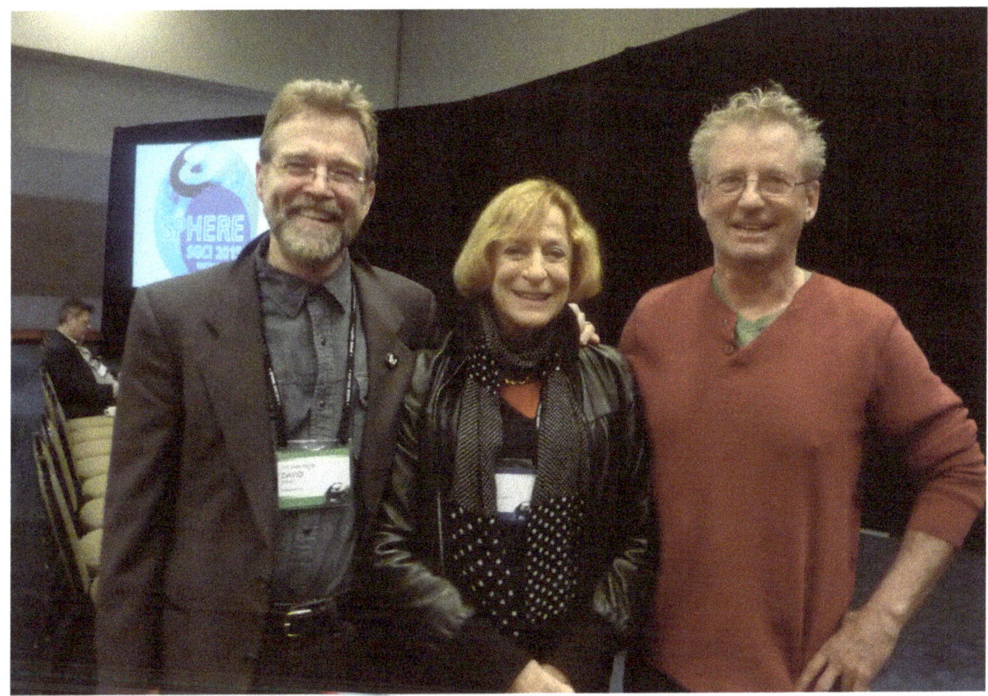

Hugh Merrill with David Jones and Ruth Weisberg at SGCI conference in Nashville, TN.
2014

Professor Hugh Merrill is a printmaker, educator, writer, community artist, poet, and stand up comedian performing at the Uptown Arts Bar in Kansas City weekly. As an artist and athlete, while playing soccer at the Maryland Institute College of Art and Yale University, he received his BFA and MFA.

He has taught Printmaking at the Kansas City Art Institute forever (1976----). He was awarded the Southern Graphics Councils Distinguished Teaching award in 2007. His artwork and prints are in over 50 Museums internationally including the Museum of Modern Art in New York. Merrill is a past President of the Jewish Museum of Kansas City and the Southern Graphics Council International. He and Adelia Ganson published Divergent Consistencies: The Studio and Community Art of Hugh Merrill, which charts 40 years of Merrill's studio and community artwork and Shared Visions: Thoughts and Experiences in Social Arts Practice, 2014.

Contact him at 816-686-8626

SHELBY
LEMON

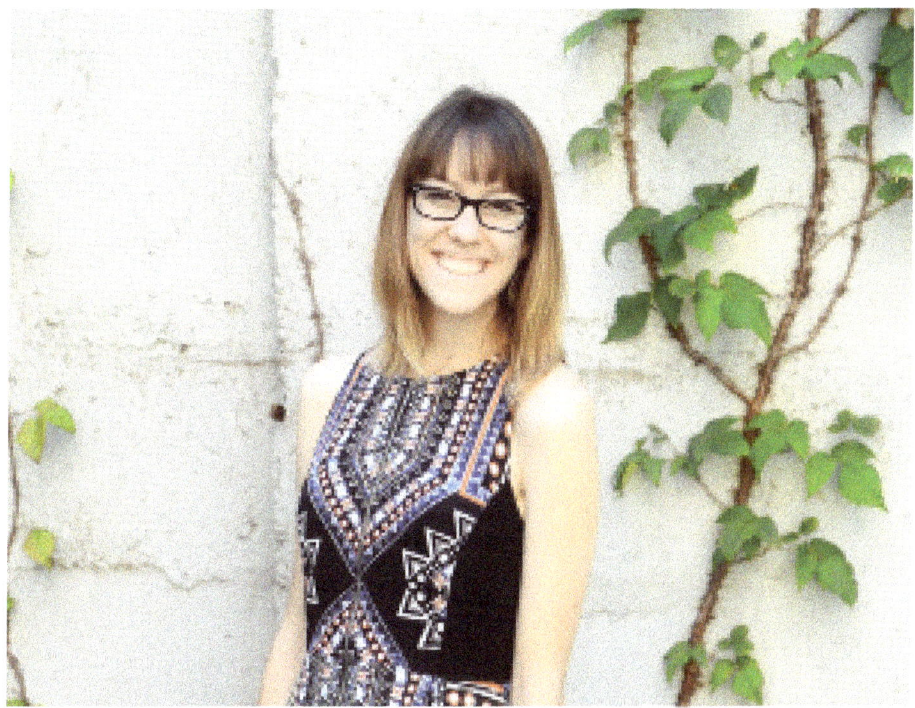

Shelby Lemon is a graphic designer, freelancer, maker and yoga instructor in the Kansas City area. She graduated from the University of Kansas in 2015 with a degree in Graphic Design. Since, she has worked in marketing, design and freelance. Projects including e-magazines, educational materials for businesses and schools, book design, branding, social media and logo design. Shelby maintains and shares a creative lifestyle with all those she meets.

Visit lovelemoncreative.com for more information.
Contact her at shelby@lovelemoncreative.com

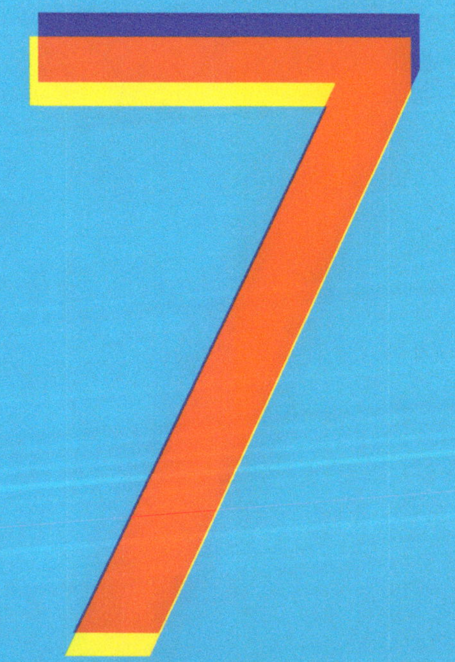

7

MEL
CHIN
DRAWS
A
SAUSAGE

, artist and printmaker Eleanor Erskine conceived and directed the printmaking and arts conference Crossing Boundaries, in Portland, Oregon, at Portland State University. Hugh Merrill was invited to give the first keynote talk. He was asked to lay out the boundary for the art world and how printmaking fits into this emerging dynamic. Rather than read a paper or do a PowerPoint presentation, Merrill decided to do a performance/lecture using the simplest of technologies, a chalkboard and a piece of white chalk. Mel Chin was also scheduled to speak, shortly after Merrill.

Here, Merrill comments on disciplinary hierarchy or the lack of it, as well as the role of the larger community and historical precedent in the support and development of artistic practice:

My thesis was based on a text from Immortality by Milan Kundera, in which he poses the following situation:

> . . . When he was a student, he imagined all painters of the world moving along the same great road; it was the royal road leading from the Gothic painters to the great Italian masters of the renaissance, and on to the Dutch painters and to Delacroix, from Delacroix to Manet, from Manet to Monet, from Bonnard (oh, how he loved Bonnard!) to Matisse, from Cezanne to Picasso. The painters did not march along this road like a group of soldiers, no, each went his own way, and yet what each of them discovered served as inspiration to the others and they all knew they were blazing a trail into the unknown, a common goal that united them all. And then suddenly the road disappeared. It was like waking up from a beautiful dream; for a while we look for the fading images until finally we realize that dreams cannot be called back. The road had

disappeared, but it remains in the souls of the painters in the form of an inextinguishable desire to "go forward." But where is "forward" when there is no longer any road? In which direction is one to look for the lost "forward"? And so the desire to go forward became the painters' neurosis; each set out in a different direction and yet their tracks crisscrossed one another like a crowd milling around in the same city square. They wanted to differentiate themselves one from the other while each of them kept discovering a different but already discovered discovery. Fortunately, people soon appeared (not artists but businessmen and organizers of exhibitions with their agents and publicists) who imposed order on this disorder and determined which discovery was to be rediscovered in any particular year. (1)

The resulting performance posed a different view of the history of contemporary art, in opposition to the timeline of progressing "isms": impressionism, post-impressionism, German expressionism, cubism, abstract expressionism and so on. Each of these achievements is a set of ideas that moves contemporary art forward, but in doing so quickly closes the book on what had recently been the cutting edge. This approach sets up an automatic contrast by attempting to make past achievements passé, and therefore of little use to the next generation of artists, who are expected to take up the torch of modernism.

If the cutting edge is all that is important, we are left with this question: How many artists can fit on that particular edge at one time? A million? No way! Maybe 100,000? Or is it 10,000? Most likely far less, perhaps 1,000 worldwide, are directly relevant to the cutting edge. Maybe not that many, maybe more; it's hard to really say.

Where does that leave the rest of us? Some are immersed in small bands of ideas, traditions and histories that have had their moment in the sun. Figurative painters, surrealists and abstract expressionists are all out there and still working, but they are no longer at the cutting edge. They are supported by their own communities of interest.

Artistic disciplines are caught in the whirlwind of aesthetic hierarchies. Some achieve momentary importance, and others are thrown aside by the mainstream critical arts community as crafts, or are pushed aside as visually unsatisfying. How many times has painting died since the end of abstract expressionism? Murdered multiple times by photography, pop art, conceptual art, happenings, performance and the list goes on.

Other disciplines have become degraded to the level of craft by critics, rich benefactors, or art mob devotees: ceramics, print, fiber and so on all rise eventually from the dead again and again to make a continuing contribution to the now, and the future soon to come.

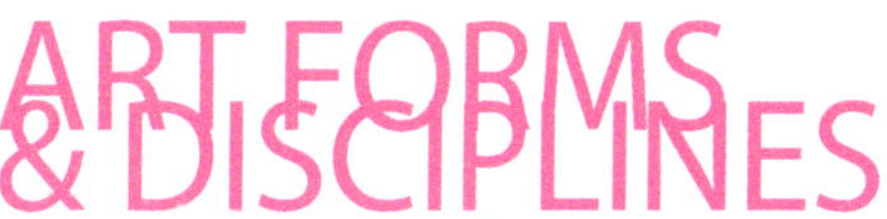

How do these art forms and disciplines survive? They survive because the community that sustains them is more powerful than theoretical relevance. Printmaking is supported by many communities, including: competitive international exhibitions, small print studios, university programs and various print groups like the Southern Graphics Council International. Yearly conferences encourage dialogue and exploration of a myriad of ideas, supporting the next generation of creative artists as they carry tradition forward, reinventing the discipline to fit their own needs. Critics often point out that we are preaching to the choir, but it's our choir and our community. Without enriching this internal support system, the medium of print, like many other areas of creativity, would shrivel and die. If we do not capture and evaluate our own history, that history will no longer exist.

Kundera's passage ends with artists stuck in the village square waiting for the art elites to tell them which discovery to rediscover. This image has the ring of truth, but art always finds new ways to move around obstruction to find not only new ground, but to resurrect the dead. Kundera's image is one of art that has lost its way, its place in society, and is merely a commercial game of high-financed collectibles for the wealthy. Kundera's image is fame based, not idea based.

Damien Hirst has assistants paint his dot paintings, which bring hundreds of thousands of dollars from wealthy collectors. Some of the Old Masters did the same thing, causing historians to guess at whose hand had actually authored the presumably single author work.

Art arises when creativity pushes against boundaries and strictures of tradition or critically defined forms of purity, absolutism or commercialism. While a group of artists waited for the news of what

ART ARISES WHEN CREATIVITY PUSHES AGAINST BOUNDARIES...

to do next, others swarmed out of the village square driven by feminism, deconstructionism, semiotics, populist and community ideals. Determined to make art with a new relevance for more people, the concerns of elite collectors, museums, and critics fell into irrelevance. Art made by the few for the few was called into question, suspended, or at least diverted momentarily by Keith Haring, David Hammonds, Judy Chicago and Barbara Kruger. Jose Gonzales-Torres replaced Kundera's cynical vision with community dialogue, ritual and direct interaction between artist and audience. These values have been around all the time hidden under the cloak and on the chalkboards of Joseph Beuys.

I wanted to show that we have potentially moved from fame-based individualism, from disciplinary hierarchies and progressive timelines, into a new world where everything has a high degree of relevance, and every creative action is a positive charge in creating a strong current of creativity for art making. There is no disagreement between the fine arts and crafts, between high fine arts and low popular arts. A scrawl on a canvas on the walls of MoMA or the marks on a commercial ad in the New York subway by Keith Haring is not only art, but an opportunity for exploring new ideas and new audiences.

Art arises when creativity

pushes against boundaries

and strictures of tradition or

critically defined forms of

purity, absolutism or

commercialism.

Everything is important.

Chicago's iconic work The Dinner Party turned artistic production on its head, drawing on a variety of crafts not seen or accepted into the aesthetic dialogue of the critical art world. Chicago brought together china painting, stitching of place mats and tablecloths with other seemingly outmoded forms of production. The Dinner Party was made collaboratively bringing to life modes of creativity that were part of women's creative history. The piece questioned the role of the artist as sole author. It was instead facilitating projects to bring together many creative hands and minds. This piece and its mode of production set a new pathway for artists to bypass the solitary confines of the genius studio.

As Chicago's Dinner Party forged connections to the hand-painting of China, the work of Kiki Smith can be seen as bound to molded or blown glass, and abstract expressionism is related to ceramics through work done by Jim Leedy or Peter Voulkos. Painting has become large silkscreen prints on canvas by way of Warhol and Rauschenberg. In fact, almost everyone connects to printmaking in some form or another. The artist no longer pursues a single discipline, instead they move freely through various disciplines, setting creative fires of energy and moving on. Sometimes, not knowing a discipline in depth becomes an advantage to take that tradition in new directions. Everything is open to change and revision and all is important and in play.

To demonstrate my ideas that art was no longer broken into hierarchies, disciplines, or a progressive time line, I drew furiously on the chalkboard, depicting batteries connected to solutions and filled with particulate matter to represent creative process and possibility. Current was added into the mixture. No matter how obscure, each element was charged and magnetically attracted to other particles bonding and creating new ideas, opportunities and chains of reactions.

I wanted to show not only was everything in play, but that the tradition of disciplinary hierarchies of fine arts and crafts held little importance. Printmaking, ceramics, china painting, even gardening no longer sat in a hierarchy where they were less valuable than painting or sculpture.

These disciplines no longer drive the creative conversation, they are merely means of creative possibilities. Painting had become merely a "craft" a process for pushing paint around for communication and expression. It no longer held a supreme theoretical position as described by Clement Greenberg. It came off the wall with the early works of Judy Pfaff, asking if the work was an installation, a 3D painting, or a sculpture. Pfaff broke the bonds of disciplinary definition. Traditional disciplines were one of many possibilities for artistic engagement, creating new hybrid investigations based on ideas and not rooted only in the material investigation and aesthetics of the "craft."

Ceramics, print, fiber, painting and photography still had value, but the value was not in their aesthetic tradition alone, or their contribution to the latest theoretical form of relevance. Their relevance existed in their community.

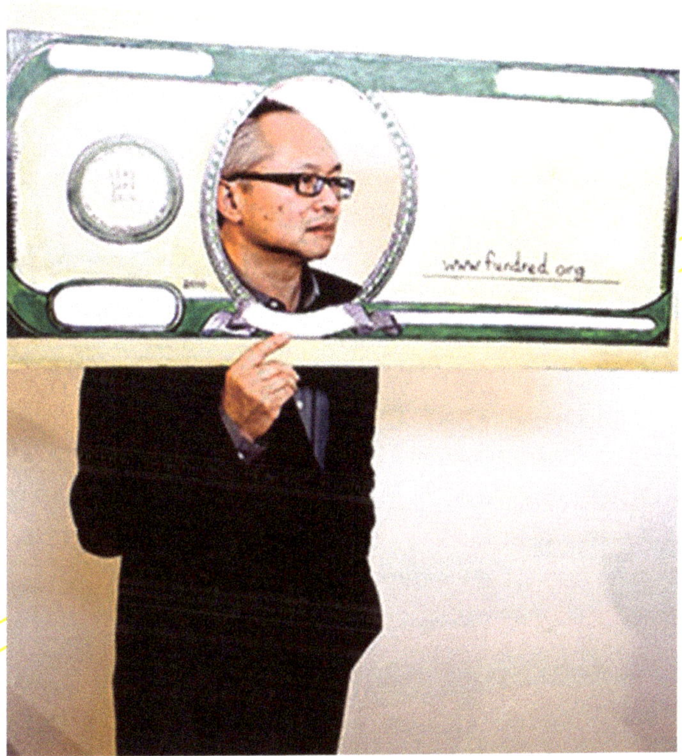

Emmett Merrill

Mel Chin at Fundred Dollar Bill Project
Leedy-Voulkos Art Center, Kansas City, Missouri
Photograph
2010

Community eclipses the theoretical relevance for a specific discipline. Theory is always a short-lived form as it changes with the society and new generations of artists. It is the community of people and their creative work, ideas, energy, and values that sustain a discipline and make it a living organism. I proposed a view in which artistic discipline is self-sufficient by creating support systems including: conferences, exhibitions and museum collections. Art of all types is open to new interactions, interpretations and uses. Print used to be limited to the hand-printed lithograph, etching, or relief print in small editions. The odd term "multiple original" was coined to describe and separate fine art prints from commercial reproductions. Posters and off-set printing were not for real artists. Then Jose Gonzales-Torres had stacks of printed offset posters produced for his installation at the Museum of Modern Art, New York, and the viewer was allowed to take one away as a gift, for free, no charge, free art!

This action was part of a broader trend of artists that were known printmakers and those outside the discipline that saw the importance of using mass communication, graphics, and copiers to produce new forms of highly accessible art that bypassed the gallery/museum system creating a new interaction directly with the audience.

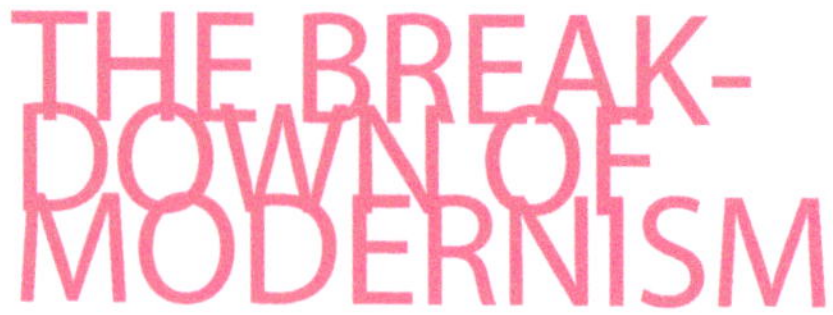

Kundera's cynical system of commercially driven, fame-based art production based on the rediscovery of past ideas to produce the seasonally new was pushed out by the deconstruction of the modernist system, feminist and community art perspectives. The new was not driven by trying to find a new way to make a painting.

With the breakdown of modernism, small sustainable, local, eccentric, community-based and social justice activities provide a rich new map for artists to navigate. Artists are not moving forward in one direction; they have taken off in many directions simultaneously, traveling the back roads of the third world and their own local communities. They do not discover new "isms" but new audiences, new forms of interaction and new hybrid creative associations. The disciplines such as print and fiber are also on these roads not defined by one set of traditions, but moving forward through growing communities of support.

My time was up and I was sure I had left the audience in a confused and perplexed state. I got the standard applause, and then looked at my highly energetic diagram on the chalkboard and began to push the board off stage to create an open space for the next speaker, Mel Chin.

Chin had prepared a PowerPoint presentation on GALA, a collective art project in which students from Georgia and California read unproduced scripts of the TV show Melrose Place and then produced art works to contradict or animate the various scenes. Mel came out on stage as I was rolling my chalkboard off with its complex maps and graphs when he stopped me. He took hold of the board and said "May I?" and rolled it back to center stage.

Chin turned to the audience and said:

> Merrill has it all wrong; it is much simpler.

He proceeded to erase my drawings as I stood off to the side out of the spotlight, listening. Mel then drew a large oval on the chalkboard. "Yes, Merrill has it all wrong. It is simple: the art world is nothing more than a sausage!"

The audience and I now recognize his drawing of an oval as a sausage and we all roar with laughter as he says:

> You see, it is a sausage and it is cookin' on the grill and it smells great; the juices are flowing, it's grilling, cooking, creating this great aroma, a great smell. Everything and everyone makes up the ingredients of the sausage, everything past and everything that is happening now. It is all cookin' inside the skin of the sausage.

He begins drawing marks representing the ingredients of the art sausage. There are printmaking, painting, new media, there are great artists too; here is Picasso, he is a big piece of fat, here is Matisse and Pollock . . . with each name mentioned, Mel makes a dot, dash, a circle, or squiggle inside the sausage. He continued:

> Merrill is here, he is tiny compared to Picasso, but he is still in there adding flavor, here is Barbara Kruger and Jenny Holzer and David Hickey. Everyone is

cookin' and adding flavor and juice to the sausage, it is real, alive . . . Then an art historian removes the sausage from the grill quickly freeze-dries it, killing it.

Chin draws a circle on the chalkboard and fills it with marks so it looks like a drawing of a pizza. "Then they cut the sausage into thin layers," he continues, "the art historian looks at the slice and says, 'Look here at this big piece of fat this is Picasso, and he is important.'"

Historians freeze the sausage to analyze the contents, and in the process the smell, taste and juiciness are lost. The aroma that makes us hungry is gone. The sausage is not cooking anymore, "So it's become a well-defined and tasteless history, frozen."

The audience roared with laughter and delight. Why? Because they see that they are all included, they are all part of a broad creative stream, part of the creative community and that they matter. They see themselves as essential ingredients contributing to the great smell and taste of the sausage/art world. They see that the living contributors of printmaking culture are all more important than critical or disciplinary relevance.

"...the art world is nothing more than a sausage!"

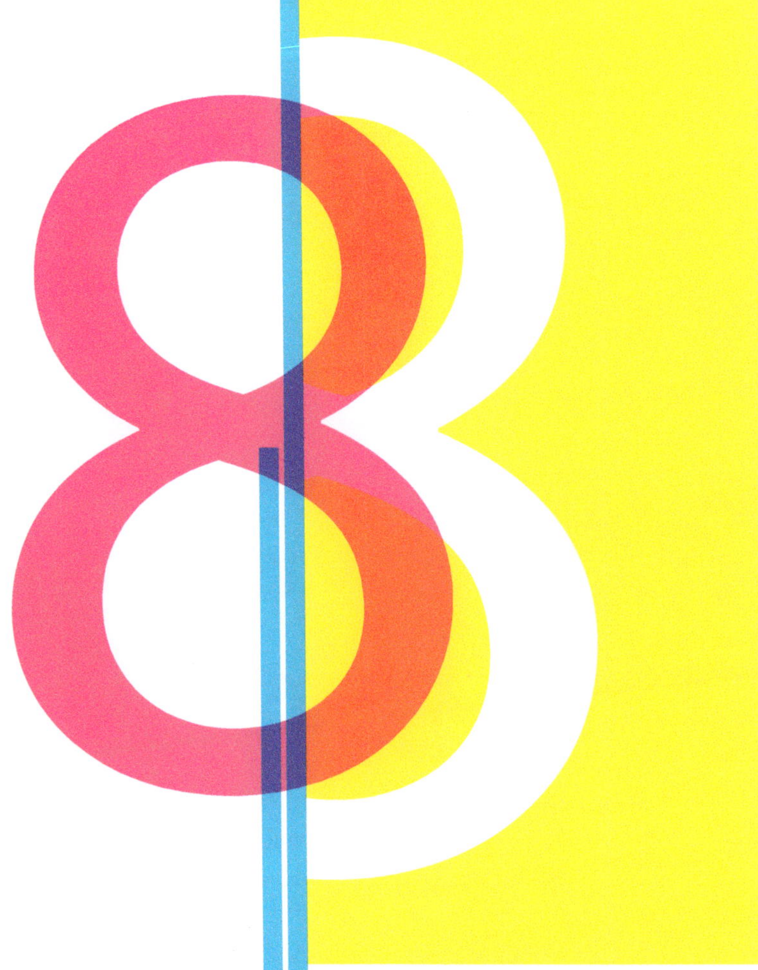

Creativity as Content

THE SEQUENTIAL PRINTS OF HUGH MERRILL

Prelude: Merrill, March 2016

Many artists, including Rauschenberg, Rembrandt, Piranesi, Cage, DeBono, Lippard, and Beuys, have continued to influence my work over the course of many years. The ideas and concepts developed from antiquity and since never lose consequence in my arc of thoughts and technical experimentation. From traditional printmaking to socially engaged arts actions, I am propelled forward by the investigation of multiple connections.

Dieter Roth's life work includes hundreds of sequential prints and multiples. When contemplating his process of creating variations of preexisting commercial images, there emerges a sense that there is more to be understood than what the image or object expresses. For instance, Roth used postcards of Trafalgar Square, in London, United Kingdom, as a starting point to create more than 100 variations of the scene. Each is new and different from previous images, and the series of altered copies tells a deeper story than the visual effect of any one of the images in the series.

What I take away is that content is found not in the expressive quality of the postcards but in the nature of creativity itself. This insight is connected to the mystical Jewish practice of Kabbalah, a belief that the universe started with a flash of light that unleashed the limitless powers of creativity into space. From this first creative act, all else has evolved. Nothing is stationary; all is changing, evolving and becoming. Old forms are transformed into new forms: biological materials, minerals, and gas into solids and solids into liquids. Everything is in a state of constant change.

Roth was a fountain of creative action, especially through his lifelong, daily ritual of making work and saving all the typically discarded scraps. He archived them while creating variations of assemblages, castings, etchings, lithographs and other works. His work has many levels of visual, social and intellectual possibilities or meanings. I find that the most profound quality is his establishment of creativity as the ultimate content of an artist's life's work.

Over decades of thinking about Roth's work and those of other artists, I have come to see more clearly that behind creative expression are mystical concepts deeply related to the very act of creativity itself. I feel that I can't really grasp these notions, but I move toward them, experiencing their reality through my own narrative.

INTRODUCTION

This interview is the result of long conversations between Merrill and noted sculptor, ceramist, and painter Jim Leedy, close friends who have reflected about life, obsession, creativity and art for many years. This interview took place in the Leedy-Voulkos Art Center and Gallery in Kansas City, Missouri, in early September 1996. Merrill's two series of sequential, black-and-white etchings were scheduled for exhibition at the Printworks Gallery in Chicago shortly after this conversation.

Both Facts of Fictions and Rules for Writing the Dead were lined up in frames along the wall in Merrill's studio. These series of images are marked by the appearance and disappearance of architectural and

JIM LEEDY

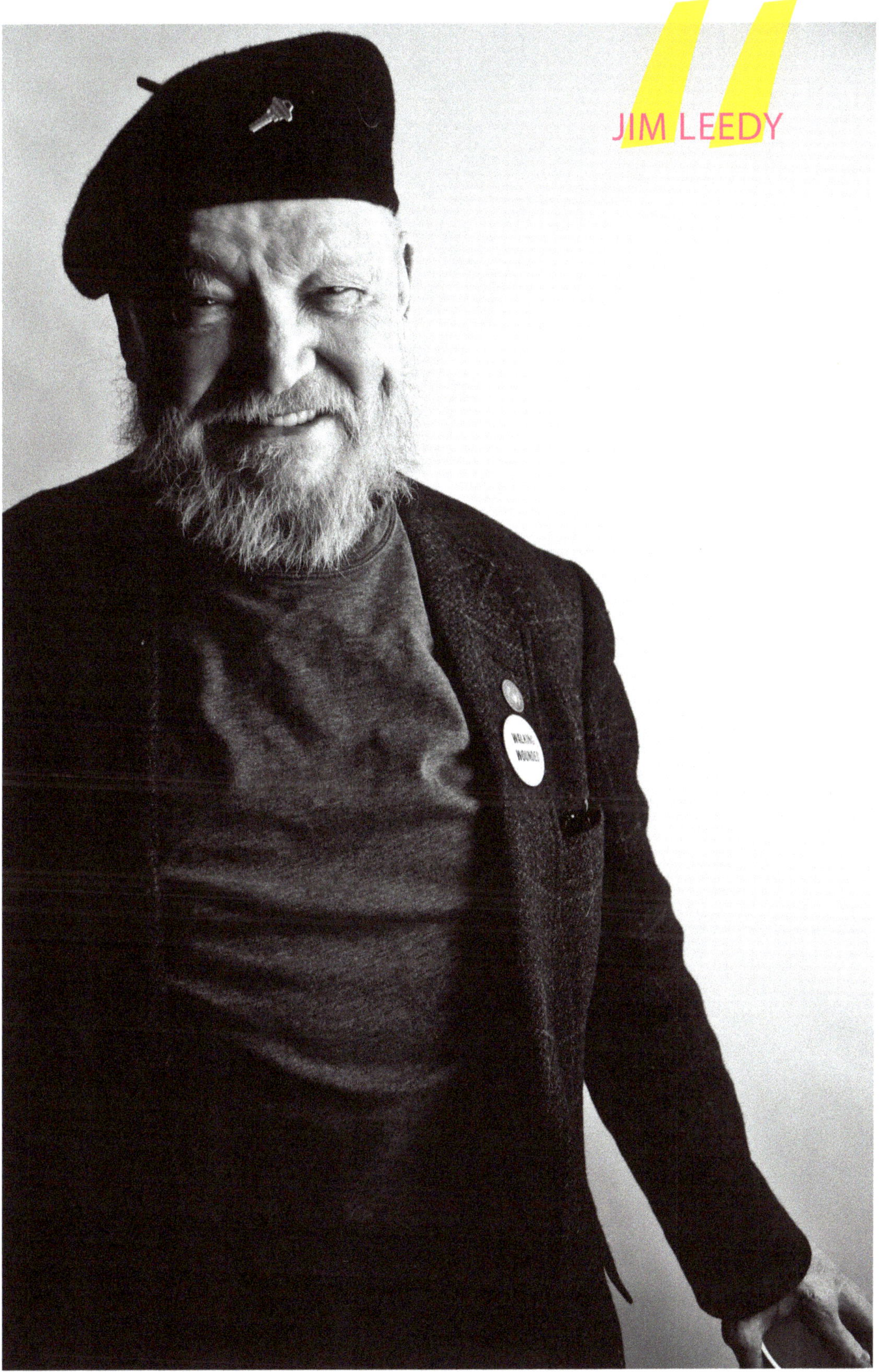

Emmett Merrill
Jim Leedy
Photograph
2013

"TECHNICALLY, WHAT I DO
CAN BE LEARNED IN THE
FIRST FEW WEEKS OF ANY
PRINTMAKING COURSE"

preindustrial forms drawn into etching plates and then scraped away, leaving only ghost images of the plates' previous state. The pieces are all 24" x 36" inches.

Leedy is one of the best-known ceramists/artists in the world. He is noted for his abstract expressionist works from the early 1950s when he and his close friend Peter Voulkos transformed the definition of ceramics. Leedy was a full professor at the Kansas City Art Institute for four decades and founded the Leedy-Voulkos Art Center and the highly energetic and successful Crossroads Arts District in Kansas City.

Merrill's use of printmaking is based on the most basic manipulations of the etching process. "Technically, what I do can be learned in the first few weeks of any printmaking course," he has said. He has taken direct drawing-based manipulation of the plate to a level of artistic investigation focused on image, sequence and content. He is uninterested in print as a multiple and does not pull editions. Instead, Merrill works the plate sequentially, pulling individual impressions and then changing the plate to create new, disturbing images. The images are

displayed in a specific order to form visual narratives with remarkable power and insight.

Leedy: For more than 10 years since the creation of the Lucky Dragon suite, you have created sequential etchings, generating images from the same plate. What is it that attracts you to this particular process?

Merrill: I have always been interested in Rembrandt's etching The Three Crosses. There are several states of this print, and each explores a different emotional possibility of the Crucifixion scene. This led me to question what comes next and led me to begin working sequentially. It is a process rooted in a dialogue with the materials. The plate becomes a memory surface. In accordance with its basic nature, the sequential process points out the infinite possibilities of change and is a test of the finite lifespan of the etching plate. Creativity and ideas are continuous, but materials are finite and concrete. It is the dialogue between the two that is at the heart of this work.

Leedy: Most printmakers create editions. They develop the matrix by proofing it until it reaches the image they are after and then pull an edition. You pull one print, then change the plate to create the next image. So, what's going on here?

Merrill: Jim, it's much like your own attitude toward ceramics, the way you consciously throw out the rules to find what works for you. The sequential process suits my creative purpose as it means that each day's work is both an independent statement and a part of a larger narrative. The plate is a surface that leaves traces of past activities, so new ideas and images are altered by the information that has gone before. At some point, the space created by the surface of the plate takes on the depth, complexity and contradictions of my thinking.

Leedy: What do you mean when you say that the etching plate is a memory surface?

Merrill: For me, the etching plate is a concrete and tangible memory surface because the act of physical manipulation references the mechanics of memory itself. The plate records an act of drawing, and through the abrasiveness of the etching process, that action is sublimated, resulting in a ghost image. With each change in the plate, the present is haunted by remnants of the past. Like memory, we see through our own past experiences, so the image I am working on at any time is changed through the past manipulations of the plate. I feel that the process is very close to the way real memory works.

Leedy: Memory seems to be a driving force in your work, but your work is not specifically autobiographical. How do you perceive and use memory?

Merrill: First off, memory is not organized like in a library or computer. Information is not filed away in memory for instant, future recall. We do not predetermine what will be remembered or when it will be recalled. Images flow across the surface of my memory, and recall is often a matter of associations that can be aroused by a smell, an object, or a sound. At this point in my life, I am not interested in autobiographical storytelling, but I am very interested in the way my memory can create an infinite number of associated, meaningful images. When I work sequentially while manipulating the matrix, I obtain access to a level of knowledge that is not available through analytical and logical methods of thought. The process allows me to bring to light information that is seemingly important yet far away.

Leedy: You see memory as intuitive, as fluid. You seem less concerned with analytical communication than expression. What are your feelings about the viewer, communication and content?

Merrill: Communication is an interesting word as its meaning has been reduced to sound bites in popular culture. I do not wish to speak to the viewer in simple, iconographic language. I think highly of the intelligence of the viewer. My images and their sequence are meant to provide the viewer with the space for prolonged speculation and a return to personal memory. The works act as a process for viewers to recognize their own perceptions, to speculate on meaning based on their experiences and the knowledge that they bring to the viewing experience.

Content is mistaken for understanding. When I look at certain works of art, I realize that something profound has come into being, but the moment I try to break it down, to dissect it, the meaning retreats. Analysis is both the apex and the burden of Western thought. To understand and to know are quite different things because knowing is complete; it is physical, as well as mental. I am trying to communicate a sense of knowing to the viewer, an intersection of physical and mental gestures organized in a narrative sequence.

Leedy: The images in The Rules for Writing the Dead are of North American Indian fish traps and baskets. These objects, through a sequence of four or five impressions, dissolve into chaos, then to a gray, undefinable, Oriental space. Is this a correct reading of the work?

Merrill: I am interested in the fluidity of images in a stage of unraveling progression. I am interested in placing objects in a space that is receding and momentary. The object is always confronted by change—from the outside and from the unavoidable entropy of the object itself. The basket images are from engravings of Indian baskets. This is important to their understanding. They are already one step removed, turned into scientific information, and I continue that process of change and absorption through the etching process.

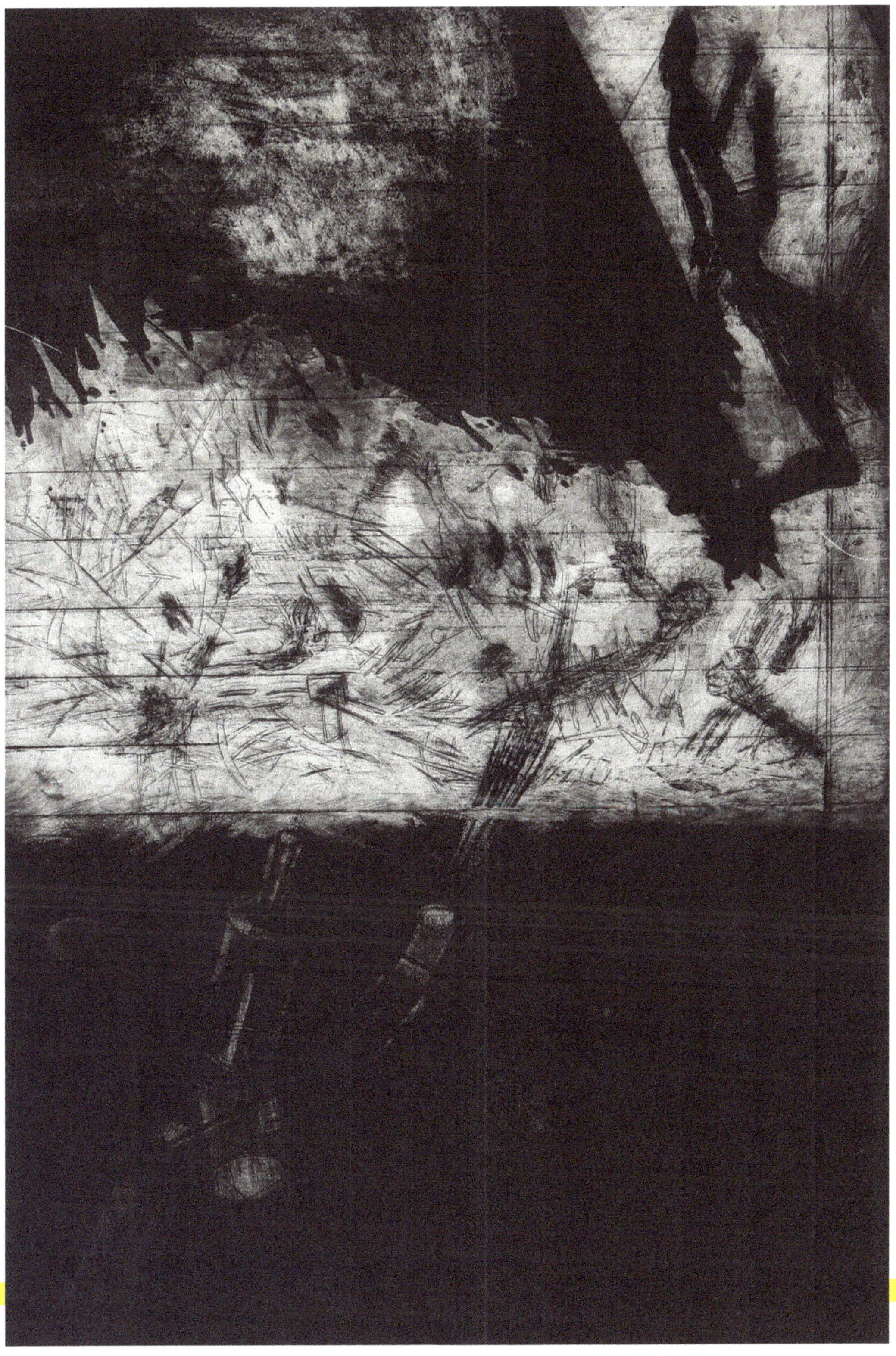

Hugh Merrill
Factory Outlet
from the Facts of Fictions suite
Etching
24′ x 36′
1990-2000

Leedy: The ongoing series Facts of Fictions begins with a large, unraveling form seemingly made of a basket-like material. Can you talk a little about these impressions?

Merrill: This series has gone on for several years and is intended to be continued indefinitely. I have gone through a number of zinc plates in working on this series. Again, the individual images and the complete narrative speak to the nature of fluidity, change and motion. The series begins with an impossible dirigible; without the ability for self-direction, the form is torn apart from its interior. This leads to images of male warrior heads and soldiers who fought with the French Marines in Vietnam, disembodied heads floating, like Mao in the Yellow River, with no arms or hands, as the heads dissolve into a debris field of cultural clutter and, finally, into a series of hands.

Leedy: What comes next?

Merrill: (Laughter) The next image, of course!

Leedy: You are working on a project with French artist Christian Boltanski. What draws you to his work?

Merrill: I am helping to create a collaborative installation between Boltanski and residents of the metro area of Kansas City, Missouri. The project Our City: Ourselves invites folks from Kansas City to bring their family photos and other memorabilia to the museum and make Xerox copies of them and then pin the photocopies to the gallery wall. Boltanski is currently constructing an exhibition sponsored by the Kemper Museum and the Museum Without Walls. The aspects of his work that interests me are his ideas about memory, appearance and disappearance. He contemplates the idea that the past is a form of death and that remembrance can be stimulated and expanded by artifacts and other specific objects.

The works are not didactic, so the perceived meaning resides in the viewer's response. Grand subjects, such as death, with historical references, such as the Holocaust, are trademarks of his work, but somehow, he avoids making them sentimental by creating distance. These are the qualities that drew me to become involved in the project. It is very interesting to turn the Kemper Museum of Contemporary Art over to everyday folks and have their lives and family memories in the building.

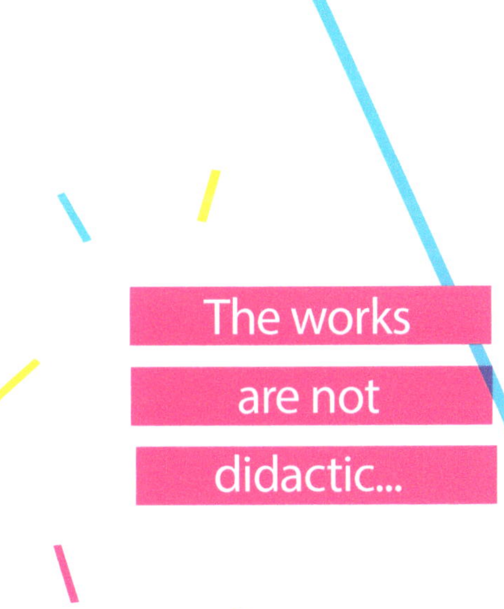